D0984048

Media Effects on Voters

A Panel Study of the 1992 Presidential Election

John William Cavanaugh

University Press of America, Inc.
Lanham • New York • London

University Press of America,® Inc.
4720 Boston Way
Lanham, Maryland 20706

3 Henrietta Street
London, WC2E 8LU England

Library of Congress Cataloging-in-Publication Data

Cavanaugh, John William.
Media effects on voters : a panel study of the 1992 presidential
election / John William Cavanaugh.
p. cm.
Includes bibliographical references and index.
1. Presidents--United States--Election--1992. 2. Mass media--
Political aspects--United States. 3. Communication in politics--
United States. 4. Advertising, Political--United States. I. Title.
JK526 1992n   324.973'0928--dc20   95-8626 CIP

ISBN 0-8191-9942-7 (cloth: alk: paper)

Dedication

FOR MIKE VENTRESCA

Michael A. Ventresca, a popular political idealist, activist, and lawyer was killed on a bright Sunday morning at the end of 1985 when a driver, drunk and on drugs, crashed into his car while he waited at a red light in Boston. He died almost instantly.

The Michael A. Ventresca Scholarship was established at UMass Boston in 1986 to honor the spirit of public service that Mike demonstrated throughout his short life. Mike devoted his life to politics and government, not only because he found it fun, but because he believed in the promise of democracy. Mike Ventresca was the person who first inspired my interest in the presidential election process. This research project on the 1992 presidential campaign is dedicated to his memory.

For further information concerning the Michael A. Ventresca Scholarship, contact: The Director of Alumni Affairs & Planned Giving, University of Massachusetts at Boston, 100 Morrissey Blvd., Boston, MA 02125-3393, or call (617) 287-5393.

Contents

Foreword

John Cavanaugh's *Media Effects On Voters: A Panel Study Of The 1992 Presidential Election,* is must reading for students of political campaigns, campaign communications, journalists, media managers, and citizens wanting to know if "in-your-face," attack journalism" influences voters' decisions in a presidential election. Using a multiple-method research case study approach to track the reaction of a panel of voters from July to November 1992, citizens of a capital city in a "Vital South" state, to campaign communication in the local and national news media, Cavanaugh finds in repeated interviews multiple mentions of 14 "attack topics" by panelists. One in five panelist recalling "attack items" in the news media, change voting intentions (from Perot to Clinton). Cavanaugh's exhaustive content analysis of campaign coverage in the city's dominant newspaper and television station, and on ABC, CBS and NBC nightly newscasts, from July through November, shows as much as 40 percent of the coverage of Bush in July, for example, was "attack journalism" (e.g., focused on the President's "shut up" remark to POW-MIA families).

Larry Sabato, Kathleen Jamieson, Thomas Patterson, the Presidential Campaign Study Group at The Freedom Forum Media Studies Center, The Times Mirror Center for People and the Press, and others, have called our attention to the transforming effect "in-your-face," "attack journalism," is having on politics. As Patterson notes in his contribution to The Freedom Forum's special Media Studies Journal issue on "The Presidency in the New Media Age," the press since Vietnam and Watergate have come to dislike politics and politicians and political reporters have come to rely on political opponents as sources for discrediting the claims of candidates. Patterson argues that the substitution by news organizations of an "attack journalism" style of reporting for investigative reporting means that democracy is not well served because press cynicism erodes the public support needed by Presidents to lead, and it causes Presidents to avoid encounters with journalists who are the conduit through which Presidents are able to provide vital information to the public (Thomas E. Patterson, "Legitimate Beef — The Presidency and a Carnivorous Press," *Media Studies Journal,* 8:2 [Spring 1994], 21-27).

Cavanaugh's combination of a pre-screening mail questionnaire, in-depth interviews over time with a panel of registered voters, and content analysis of local and national media coverage of the election, result in a richer understanding of the impact of "attack journalism" on voting choice.

His replication of Doris Graber's Evanston panel study provides as well an effective design for assessing the effects of news organizations' efforts to empower democratic institutions, as Knight-Ridder newspapers in Charlotte and Wichita have tried to do in their coverage of presidential campaigns.

Cavanaugh's approach serves as a useful model for a research agenda in studying the 1996 presidential election, a design that can be implemented by researchers, media organizations and public interest groups in other communities in the "Vital South," and other regions of the country.

Lowndes F. Stephens
Associate Dean, Graduate Studies and Research
College of Journalism and Mass Communications
University of South Carolina
STEPHENS-LOWNDES@SCAROLINA.EDU

Acknowledgements

Dr. John Ambacher at Framingham State College helped me to embark on this journey by initiating my academic interest in political science. All my teachers and friends at the John W. McCormack School of Public Affairs at the University of Massachusetts kept me on course. Then, I decided to cast off to a new port, South Carolina, in order to see and study politics in the "Vital South."

I wish to thank several professors from the University of South Carolina for all their assistance to me: Dr. Kenny Whitby, a skilled academic in the field of elections and voting behavior, taught me long ago that quiet persistence and working after hours are the keys to academic success. Dr. Rick Stephens from the School of Journalism and Mass Communication has provided me with constant encouragement and enthusiasm for my research interests. Dr. David Whiteman offered his time, patience, and special expertise in media and politics. Dr. Blease Graham, also graciously took time from his busy schedule in order to review my work from the standpoint of a highly respected scholar in the field of voting behavior in South Carolina. Finally, Dr. Ann Bowman, also made special arrangements in her schedule in order to help review my research.

Other members of USC's Department of Government and International Studies warrant special mention. Sandra Hall, Becky Deaton, and Lori Joy have always provided me support, encouragement, and comic relief during my time here at USC. Dr. Hal Birch adeptly scheduled me into many varied teaching assignments so that I could pay my rent, buy groceries, and fend off at least some of my creditors. My friend and colleague, Dr. Jeff Greene, consistently helped with telephone "sanity checks" even when he moved to his new job at the University of Montana.

Thanks to a small grant from Dr. David Claybrook and the Graduate Council Fellowship, I was able to purchase five months of national television news indexes and abstracts from the Vanderbilt Television News Archive.

I also need to thank Michelle Cromer at the Richland County Board of Voter Registration for her kind help with the voter registration lists for the city of Columbia. Likewise, my appreciation goes to Cristina Mohr of WIS-TV News, who helped me with my local television news content analysis data. I wish to acknowledge the assistance of Michael Thigpen, an M.P.A. graduate from USC, who provided skilled consultation on the statistical charts and graphs in Chapter 4. Also, Olin Jenkins of Jenkins Typography in Columbia deserves credit for helping to put the manuscript into the proper book format.

I also wish to acknowledge the helpful comments of Dr. Stephanie Larson of Dickenson College and Dr. Marilyn Yale from the University of Houston. Both reviewed parts of my research on "The Mass Media and Politics" panel at the 1992 Southern Political Science convention in Atlanta. Likewise, I wish to thank Dr. Robert Savage of the University of Arkansas and Dr. Patricia A. Hurley of Texas A&M University. These two fine scholars provided helpful critiques of my work on "The Media and Presidential Elections" panel at the 1993 Southwestern Social Science Association meeting in New Orleans. Dr. Peggy Conway of the University of Florida and Dr. John Haskell of Drake University deserve thanks for reviewing my ideas while serving on the "Presidential Nominations and Primaries" panel at the 1994 Southern Political Science Association Meeting in Atlanta.

I am deeply thankful to all the Columbia residents who took the time to return my mail questionnaire and I am grateful beyond words to the eighteen panel members who invited me into their homes and offices or who spent time with me in coffee shops and libraries during the course of the 1992 general election. As I stated in my cover letter to you in May of 1992, I still believe that "your opinion does count" and that your participation in this project may help to improve the way the press covers Presidential elections in the future.

I also want to thank Dr. Judy Small, Dr. Jan Love, Honors College Dean Peter Sederberg, and Melanie P. Carter of the English Department at the University of Alabama for providing calm waters and safe harbors during the final stages of this marathon project. Lastly, I wish to thank Michelle Harris and Helen Hudson of University Press of America, Inc. I sincerely appreciate all the time and effort you both put into this project.

Introduction

This study is an intensive microanalysis of mass media effects on a panel of eighteen voters from Columbia, South Carolina, during the 1992 presidential election. Given the rise of media "feeding frenzies" that now manifest themselves in modern presidential campaigns, I thought it would be appropriate to revisit the panel study approach taken by Doris Graber in *Processing The News* in order to determine how 1992 voters cope with the phenomenon of "attack journalism" in an age of televised campaigns.

Social scientists initially feared that information from new communications devices such as radio and television would have a "magic bullet effect" on citizens. However, early studies in this area by Lazarsfield and Berelson found media effects to be relatively insignificant. Concerns of a volatile electorate easily swayed by new media technologies subsided in favor of the notion that voters resembled uninformed robots responding simply to partisan and social cues. This view of the electorate was challenged by scholars such as V.O. Key, who discovered evidence that voters did exercise rational evaluation of candidates and their policy proposals. More recent research involving political information processing by Graber, Jamieson, and Popkin suggests that voters organize election information by means of cognitive frameworks or schemas. When individuals consume news items, new information can be absorbed or abandoned. If it is absorbed, it can confirm past beliefs, change previously held beliefs, or lead to new thinking.

The purpose of this study is to build upon voter information processing theory and to add to the body of scholarly studies that examine both the forces that create news content and the effect of media content. Since previous research has found that citizens are exposed to a plethora of news information and that voters usually have poor recall of campaign news, this investigation addresses concerns that voters may react to attack journalism in a manner similar to the original magic bullet theory. The two key research questions are as follows: Do attack news items reach all voters regardless of political interest or media access? Does attack journalism affect individual vote choice? If the magic bullet effect holds true, attack journalism will make contact with all voters, and voters will abandon support for candidates who become the objects of the attack.

In order to address these issues, the methodology in this study allowed for a group of voters and their voluminous news sources to be tracked over time during the 1992 presidential election. In other words, echoing V.O. Key, we can see if the voters "stand-pat" with their early favorite or "switch"to another candidate later in the campaign. Separate interviews with each panelist were conducted every two weeks during the months of July, August, September, October, and November of 1992. Hence, based on the interview responses, we get both a long-term glimpse of voters in the decision-making process and an insight into how attack news items affect their vote choice. In order to examine how 1992 election news items affected specific groups of voters, the eighteen panelists in this study were divided into four groups depending upon their interest in politics and their access to the media: 1. High interest in politics/easy access to the media, 2. High interest in politics/difficult access to the media, 3. Low interest in politics/easy access to the media, 4. Low interest in politics/difficult access to the media.

The findings of this study substantiate Key's original supposition that voters exercise rational evaluation of Presidential candidates. Likewise, this research confirms Graber's thesis that voters may take information gathering shortcuts; but, overall, citizens cope fairly well with the overwhelming proliferation of news in today's society. The results of this study indicated that attack journalism tends to catalyze the interest of voters in each group relatively uniformly; however, such items do not uniformly affect vote choice. With the backdrop of the 1992 economic recession, the panelists in this study based their vote choices primarily on each candidate's economic policy prescriptions for the nation rather than media feeding frenzies concerning their personal life. Future research should focus on voter information processing of attack journalism during elections that occur at the time of more sound economic conditions.

Chapter 1

The Growing Role of the Media in American Presidential Elections

According to Flanigan and Zingale, the "central focus on research on American political behavior is vote choice, especially presidential vote choice. No other single form of mass political activity has the popular interest or analytic significance that surrounds the selection of a president every four years."[1] The literature on this topic contains several contrasting viewpoints regarding the determinants of vote choice and the overall sophistication of voters. Moreover, since the introduction of television, scholars have had renewed interest in the area of media influences on voters. The 1988 presidential campaign flush with images of Willie Horton, Donna Rice and flag factories provided a watershed or perhaps a "waterloo" in this field with scholars, pundits, reporters, candidates, and the public at large left wondering if the American presidential selection process had devolved into what Germond and Witcover call "the trivial pursuit of the presidency."[2]

This study is an intensive microanalysis of mass media effects on a panel of eighteen voters from Columbia, South Carolina, during the 1992 presidential general election. Given the rise of media "feeding frenzies" that now manifest themselves in modern presidential campaigns, I thought it would be appropriate to revisit the panel study approach taken by Doris Graber in *Processing The News* in order to determine how 1992 voters cope with the phenomenon of "attack journalism" in the age of televised campaigns.[3]

While the number of panelists in this study is small, the approach allowed for voters and their voluminous news sources to be tracked over time. Each panelist was interviewed separately every two weeks during the months of July, August, September, October, and November of 1992. During that same time period, I conducted a content analysis on *The State* newspaper of Columbia, South Carolina and WIS-TV, the local NBC affiliate that broadcasts statewide in South Carolina. I also utilized the television news abstracts from Vanderbilt University in order to analyze national news broadcasts during the general election. Over twenty thousand newspaper and television news items were coded and placed into sixty four categories. Hence, we get both a long-term glimpse of voters in the decision-making process and an insight into how news items affect their vote choice. In other words, echoing V.O. Key, we can see if these voters "stand-pat" with their early favorite or "switch" to another candidate later in the campaign. Most importantly, we can see if specific types of news items affect voter perception of the candidates.

The remainder of this chapter will consist of a further examination of the literature regarding voting behavior, the ever changing nature of the presidential selection process, and the growing influence of the mass media on presidential elections. Chapter 2 provides a general chronological overview of the 1992 presidential campaign. Chapter 3 presents a more detailed explanation of the research setting, the panel study methodology and the news content analysis procedures. Chapter 4 reports the findings of the news media contents analysis. Chapter 5 recounts the panelist interviews. Finally, Chapter 6 discusses the implications of this research and suggests possible systemic changes that may result in an improved presidential selection process.

Early Studies Of Media Effects On Voting Behavior

As Winebrenner states, "Prior to the 1970s, studies of elections and voting behavior by political scientists paid relatively little attention to the role of the media in the United States.[4] Perhaps this is because early studies in this area by Lazarsfield and Berelson in 1940 and 1948 found media effects to be relatively insignificant.[5] Scholars believed party loyalty and general conversations about elections with family and friends better explained electoral choices. Eventually, an unfavorable portrait of voters in the United States emerged in the literature. Early fears of a volatile electorate easily swayed by new media technologies (radio initially) disappeared in favor of the notion that most voters resembled uninformed robots responding to partisan and social cues. These findings were advanced in studies during the early 1960s by Campbell, Converse and Stokes.[6] But other scholars, such as V.O. Key, challenged this orthodox view. In an examination of "new voters," "switchers," and "stand-patters" from 1936 to 1960, Key discovered evidence that voters did exercise rational evaluation of candidates and their policy proposals. Key emphatically argued against the conventional wisdom and proclaimed that "voters are not fools."[7]

Despite academic disagreements concerning the rationality of voters, there is almost universal consensus that partisanship provides the most stable and consistent predictor of voting behavior. As Flanigan and Zingale explain, an "individual's partisanship can be construed as a long-term predisposition to vote for one party or another, other things being equal."[8] However, other short-term influences such as candidate image and issues may cause voters to stray from usual party loyalty. As Sunquist states, "in each election a few deviants cross the party line to support the opposition or rebuke their own leaders."[9] But these temporary shifts in support may not fundamentally change the "basic psychological attachment" of these voters to their party organization. According to Sundquist, "For an issue to shatter a party system and create a new one, it clearly must arise from a grievance that is both broad and deep, that a large number of people feel strongly about."[10] Phillips contends that factors such as economic conditions, geography, and historical events can act as the causal factors which create shifts in party alignments.[11]

As Sundquist comments, "If there is no consensus as to where the party system is going, even among those who agree that it is headed in a new direction, there is at least a considerable degree of consensus about where it has been."[12] There is general consensus in the literature that there have been at least five major party system realignments. The first occurred in 1800 when the Jeffersonian Republicans defeated the Federalists. The second took place in 1828 when the Jacksonian Democrats seized power. The third realignment transpired in 1860 when the Republicans displaced the Whig party. The fourth happened in 1896 when the Republicans defeated the Democrats led by Williams Jennings Bryan. The fifth ensued in 1932 when Democratic Governor Franklin Delano Roosevelt defeated incumbent President Herbert Hoover. The Roosevelt coalition remained relatively stable until the 1980 election of Ronald Reagan. The rise of independent voters or "ticket-splitters" since that election has marked a new phase of mass voting behavior which political scientists have termed "de-alignment."

Phillips notes that, well before the "Reagan revolution," the Democratic party has exhibited "profound ideological cleavages," especially since the 1972 election defeat of George McGovern. He explains that the split within the Democratic party was even more pronounced than the split between mainstream Democrats and Republicans: "On one side were the key blocs of the New Deal coalition: Southerners, ethnics, and blue-collar workers. Leading the other side were the advocates of the New Politics (suburban liberals, skilled professionals, collegians) and their minority group allies."[13] Phillips and Earl and Merle Black contend that the turmoil in the Democratic base can be seen geographically. Losses of voter allegiances in the "solid" South have been costly to the party causing a "Dixie schizophrenia" in which the "South has been increasingly Republican on the national level and still substantially (conservative) Democratic in Congressional, state and local offices."[14] More recently, in many Southern states, Republicans have been successful in statewide contests and are increasingly competitive in local races.

With so many unstable clusters of voters, there is a bitter debate concerning the future of the American electorate. Some scholars argue that these clusters will coalesce into a new Republican majority in the near future. Recent Republican United States Senate special election victories in Georgia and Texas combined with the latest Republican gubernatorial wins in Virginia and New Jersey as well as a Republican mayoral win in New York help to bolster this argument. Others argue that the new Perot movement may transform into a full fledged third party and eventually displace either the Democrats or Republicans. Still others argue that the Clinton victory may signal a new majority coalition for the Democratic party. In addition, there is the possibility that de-alignment will continue and partisan allegiances will erode even further. Perhaps the 1994 midterm elections or the 1996 Presidential elections will provide more explicit clues as to the future direction of the American electorate.

A Presidential Selection Process In Constant Flux

Further complicating the debate concerning the sophistication of voters in national elections, is the ever-changing nature of the presidential election process itself and the continuing uncertainty concerning the health of American political parties. Ceaser explains that from 1789 to 1968 the presidential election process evolved into four distinct phases[15]: First from 1787 to 1796, the American chief executive emerged from the Constitutional blueprint established by the founders of the American republic. Epstein notes that this constitutional design containing a "separately elected, politically powerful chief executive" is uniquely American with "no counterpart in a parliamentary system whose chief working executive is the product of legislative elections."[16] Under the framer's original plan, the presidential election was a non-partisan process governed by an "electoral college." As Jamieson reports: "The creators of our government envisioned the electoral process as a staid, dignified activity — a few respected electors, state by state, sifting the merits of the worthiest eligibles. Something like a church council naming a new pastor, or a faculty bestowing a professorship."[17]

State legislators determined how members of this "deliberative" college would be chosen and each state was assigned a number of electors equal to the total number of United States Senators and Representatives. The candidate who received a majority of electoral college votes became president and the second place finisher became the vice president. The House of Representatives determined the winner in case of a tie vote of the electoral college.

From 1800 to 1816, the process changed. Fledgling political parties began to emerge requiring some form of nomination. During this second phase in presidential selection, a "King" Caucus of congressional leaders screened and selected competitors for the general election. James Monroe was selected by the Congressional Caucus and the Democratic Republican party dominated the political landscape. Monroe's election as President ushered in the "Era of Good Feelings."[18]

The electoral college remained intact during the King Caucus phase, but the newly passed 12th Amendment separated votes for president and vice president. In 1824, the Democratic Republican party nominated Monroe's Secretary of the Treasury, William Crawford. However, Crawford was challenged by several other candidates: John Quincy Adams, John C. Calhoun, Henry Clay, and Andrew Jackson. No candidate received an electoral college majority and the House of Representatives chose Adams to be the chief executive even though Jackson had won more popular votes. This election in 1824 marked the death of the King Caucus.[19]

Ceasar notes that from 1832 to 1908 presidential selection changed again into a third stage which he terms the "Pure Convention System." This change was sparked by a small political party known as the Anti-Masons which held the first political convention in 1831 in a

Baltimore saloon. Three months after that meeting, opponents of
Andrew Jackson met in the same location for another convention.

Seizing the trend, Jackson himself convened a Democratic
convention in order to display broad-based support for his running
mate, Martin Van Buren. Eventually, nominating conventions became
a staple of the national election process. Lowi explains that this new
procedure was a fundamental change. It essentially cut Congress off
from the presidential election process establishing for the first time,"an
institutionalized *real* separation of powers."[20] These newly fashioned
political conventions became independent self-governing bodies with
their own rules of conduct. State and local officials selected delegates
and presidential aspirants required a 2/3's majority of these delegates
to win the nomination.

From 1924 to 1968, a fourth system emerged with many similarities to the process we have in place today. Progressive reformers
such as Robert LaFollette of Wisconsin and Hiram Johnson of
California decried the convention system comprised of delegates
controlled by party bosses and argued for popular election of delegates.
These efforts by progressive reformers paid off. Presidential selection
eventually became a mixed hybrid of primaries and conventions.
However, this process was a gradual and uneven progression. For
example, the number of presidential primaries initially increased from
four in 1908 to twenty-six in 1926.

After World War I, the number of states holding primaries
declined rapidly. In addition, until 1968, politicians who participated in
presidential primaries were considered "weak" candidates attempting
to circumvent the will of the party bosses. Thus, at first, the reformers
modified the selection process, but they failed to change the outcome.
Nominations still rested in the hands of the party leadership, because
the majority of the delegates at the convention were still under the
control of party officials.

Wayne argues that the primary process only became an
institutionalized format for all contenders when underdog primary
participants such as Dwight Eisenhower in 1952, John Kennedy in
1960, and Richard Nixon in 1968, began to succeed in winning the
presidency.[21] Hence, the number of primaries increased again from
1968 to 1980. More importantly, due to party reforms, the characteristics of convention delegates changed dramatically. Most of the
delegates to the national conventions were elected through the primary
process as opposed to being hand-picked by party leaders. Likewise,

candidates only needed a simple majority of these delegates to win the nomination.

The Van Buren Model Vs. The Woodrow Wilson Model

This gradual transformation of the characteristics of convention delegates had a distinct effect on both the conduct of the campaign and the outcome of the process. In fact, the evolutionary nature of the American presidential selection process itself has helped to spawn the rise in influence of the mass media in our modern presidential campaigns. Ceasar further suggests that this evolution of presidential selection should be seen as a battle between two very different national election models[22]. During the "Pure Convention" stage discussed earlier, presidential elections operated under the "Van Buren" or "party-dominance" model. Despite being removed from the early nomination process, the public at large still had strong party identification and a generally favorable attitude toward party organizations. However, with the dawn of the progressive movement, presidential selection shifted to the "Woodrow Wilson" model. In this model, "candidate-centered" campaigns arose and nominations became the responsibility of "interested amateurs" by means of caucuses and primaries. Under the Wilson model, the electorate is theoretically "responsive" to current issues and open to constant political change, but the public at large has either an ambivalent or hostile attitude toward political parties. With this model, as Burns explains, "The average officeholder hates a strong party, unless she or he happens to control it. That hate is somewhat logical. Most politicians in America gain high office not through party organizations, as we have seen, but through their personal organizations. They win nominations, not by working through the party structure, but by winning a primary election. Of course vote seekers are greedy and will accept all the party support they can get in the general election."[23] As Epstein notes, "A president whose nomination rests on popular support in primaries and the news media appears more decisively separated than his predecessors from party organizations and party officeholders."[24]

The Media Fill The Vacuum Left By Party Organizations

Salmore and Salmore explain that the emergence of the media is a direct result of the decline of the "party-centered" campaign and the rise of the "candidate-centered" campaign.[25] Moreover, this change is a relatively recent phenomenon as television did not cover presidential campaigns extensively until 1960[26]. As Schram comments, "Ever since the television age of politics was born in the 1952 campaign of Dwight Eisenhower versus Adlai Stevenson, the ability to use the medium has been increasingly essential to electoral success."[27] Once again there is concern among scholars that the introduction of new media technology (this time television) has radically altered the political process. Pomper explains that as the role of political parties decline, the importance of television increases: "Party organizations have been displaced by candidate organizations and the mass media"[28]. Likewise, Patterson observes, "Today's presidential campaign is essentially a mass media campaign"[29]

This "displacement" of party organization presents troubling questions concerning the character of modern democracy in the United States. As Gillespie notes, "Mass media, especially television, also have come to intrude into the domain formerly commanded by the Republican and Democratic parties. By virtually all accounts from political scientists, mass media today have replaced major parties as the principle intercessories or links between voters and candidates in presidential elections."[30] This new arrangement would most certainly have proven troubling to E.E. Schattschneider who stated over fifty years ago:

> The rise of political parties is indubitably one of the principle distinguishing marks of modern government. The parties, in fact, have played a major role as makers of democratic government. It should be stated flatly at the outset that this volume is devoted to the thesis that the political parties created democracy and that modern democracy is unthinkable save in terms of the parties.[31]

Does this shift from a party-centered presidential campaign to a candidate-centered one make modern democracy "unthinkable?" If political parties are essential to modern American democracy, then why did the framers fail to incorporate party structure into the Constitutional plan? Since Madison in *Federalist #10* was openly biased *against* organized "factions" in the new nation, what is it about "modern" democracy that requires such organizations? As James MacGregor Burns comments, "Whether the Framers were diabolically clever in their anti-party strategy or whether they frustrated parties merely as part of their broader effort against factions in general, the effect was the same — radically to alter the balance of fission and fusion in American politics."[32] In *A Preface to Democratic Theory*, Dahl explains that the ideal election allows all individuals to possess identical facts about political choices during the "prevoting period."[33] In the modern presidential selection process, political parties helped to fill that role. Over time, parties developed into clearinghouses for election information and widespread citizen participation. They also became a mechanisms for government accountability. As Alger explains:

> The underlying key point is that most people cannot make monitoring government and various candidates in elections a full-time job. For popular control of government to work, the public must have some help in sorting out the choices. For government itself to work in a coherent fashion, and for the public to hold officers accountable for the general direction of government, there must be a force that politically organizes government activity and that can be held collectively responsible for government actions. That force has traditionally been the political parties.[34]

Sorauf and Beck explain, there are three essential parts to American political parties: the party organization, the party in government, and party in the electorate[35]. Traditionally the party organization in the electoral process has been the link between the party in the electorate and the party in government. However, as we observed earlier, since the Constitution provides no framework for political parties to select a standard bearer, the nomination process has been a hodgepodge of constant rule changes and reforms making American party organizations an unstable and inconsistent link with the electorate. As Burns explains, after the chaos in 1968, the Democratic party initiated a series of commissions to critically examine the nomination process: the McGovern-Fraser Commission, the 1972 Mikulski Commission, the 1976 Winograd Commission, and the 1980 Hunt Commission. However the reforms generally missed the mark, "Carried along by the anti-establishment spirit of the late 1960s and early 1970s, the reformers tried to cleanse the presidential primary system of its exclusive and elitist elements rather than containing it. Still influenced by old reformist and progressive fears of boss-controlled caucuses and back-room deals, they did not seize the opportunity to regenerate the one alternative to media-oriented, money-dominated presidential primaries — an alternative that was not new, but had had a vital part in the expansion of American democratic politics. That alternative was the national convention."[36]

Ironically, when the major political parties shifted to direct primaries in an effort to further democratize the nomination process, they inadvertently created a vacuum in which an unelected, for-profit entity became the intermediary between voter and candidate. As Phillips comments, "Over all, the Communications Revolution has been the central factor in undercutting the get out the vote function of party organizations, straight-ticket voting, and traditional adherence."[37] Without the "peer review" of past party elites, citizens must now depend on individual campaigns and the media for political information. Pomper highlights the essential flaw with this new arrangement, "The dilemma is that both sources of information have other goals beyond contributing to democratic discussion. For campaigns, the primary goal is to win. For the commercial media, the primary goal is to attract viewers or sell newspapers."[38]

According to Entman, "The press is supposed to enhance democracy both by stimulating political interest and by providing the specific information citizens need to hold government accountable."[39] But does the modern press enhance democracy? Graber frames the fundamental question: "Is democracy based on the notion of a well-informed, civic-minded citizenry, possible, or is it a pipe dream or distant goal that cannot be reached with the current communications practices?"[40] As Lichtenberg comments, television has altered the political landscape, "It personalizes politics: public officeholders and office-seekers who in the past would have been quite remote to the ordinary person are now living breathing human beings. That by itself arouses our curiosity about them."[41] Presidential candidates are now "stars of the news, who like the star hired to lure us to a film are intended to draw the mass audience to the news channel."[42] As Barber comments:

> The transformation of the election from an event to a saga set the stage for the appearance of new militant vocabularies, as campaign organizations maneuvered over the expanded primary terrain, month after month, exercising their logistics and strategies to build

momentum and avoid erosion. Campaign maneuver itself became the featured story; the Presidential implications of what the candidates were saying faded into the distance. Horserace imagery gave way to Parcheesi politics — war against the scoreboard — a new game of expectations and scenarios and surprises played as vigorously by the candidates as by the press reporting them.[43]

In *The Sound of Leadership,* Hart calls the campaign trail "the psychodrama of American politics in which long days 'harden' the candidates in the blast furnace of media scrutiny so that they are transformed into presidential steel."[44] However, does the furnace temper each candidate evenly? In the competition for audience share does the media focus too much on what Hart calls "the odd indiscretion, the misdelivered line, and the inverted fact?"[45] This magnified media focus is what Sabato calls "attack journalism."[46] This type of journalistic "feeding frenzy" is dangerous because it may upset our basic function of political learning.

Voters normally organize information by means of cognitive frameworks or "schemas."[47] When individuals consume news items, new information may be absorbed or abandoned. If it is absorbed, it can lead to new thinking, confirm past beliefs, or change previously held beliefs. However, before such information affects voter perceptions, the individual's interest must be sparked. Newman contends that such learning is a cyclical process which is "catalyzed by a critical mass of news coverage." For the potential voter "information stimulates interest which stimulates the accumulation of further information."[48] Once a story reaches critical mass: "conflict escalates in a rising action, the high point of tension, which is followed by an unraveling or resolution."[49]

The Evolution Of Attack Journalism

But many scholars argue that this conflict and tension represented in press accounts is not new and that America has always had attack journalism. As Freund states, "Our elections have often been exercises in slander; the great issues of the day have often been beside the point. Odious campaigns are a national tradition, and so is complaining bitterly about them."[50] Similarly, professor Douglas Wilson tracks early manifestations of today's media fixation on "character issues" to past press coverage of Thomas Jefferson. For example, Jefferson endured press attacks for an attempt during his youth to court his neighbor's wife. Moreover, James Callender, a Richmond news editor disgruntled over being passed over by Jefferson for the postmaster general job, spread unsubstantiated rumors of Jefferson's siring of illegitimate children with his slave, Sally Hemings.[51]

Before the 1832 elections, newspapers printed brutal reports denigrating Andrew Jackson's parents. Articles identified his mother as a prostitute and his father as a mulatto.[52] This type of press conduct surely motivated Alexis de Tocqueville to write: "The journalists of the United States possess a vulgar turn of mind. The characteristics of the American journalist consist in an open and coarse appeal to the passions of his readers; he abandons principles to assail the characters of individuals, to track them into private life and disclose all their weaknesses and vices."[53]

In the 1840 election, *The Baltimore Republican* attacked William Henry Harrison's fitness to be president claiming he would be better suited on a military pension in a log cabin with casks of hard cider to keep him happy.[54] However, the Harrison forces were clever enough to turn these attacks around into positive images of a humble military leader close to the common folk. Other press reports claimed Harrison had failing health. The Harrison campaign again countered by putting the candidate on an extensive personal tour around the country. However, the health reports might have had a degree of veracity as Harrison died in office shortly after the election.

Press reports preceding the 1860 campaign claimed Abraham Lincoln was an illegitimate son. Later reports attacked his wife and accused his son of profiteering on the war. In 1888, there were widely circulated stories and political cartoons depicting Grover Cleveland's fathering of an illegitimate son. However, these past stories, some of them outright falsehoods, did not keep Washington, Jefferson, Jackson, Harrison, Lincoln and Cleveland from attaining the White House. Crouse claims that presidential campaign coverage "began to settle into a neat and comfortable science around the time of Theodore Roosevelt."[55] Once elected Roosevelt installed the first White House pressroom, provided the first campaign press schedules, and periodically leaked information to trusted members of the press.[56] Over time, modern journalists began to refrain from attacks and became lulled into what Sabato terms a period of "lap dog" journalism.[57] According to Crouse, who researched press coverage of the 1972 campaign, reporters formed a hierarchical pack. This "pack journalism" provided elements of "groupthink" in which editors discouraged reports that were not confirmed by other major reporters or wire stories:

> The most experienced national political reporters, wire men, and big-paper reporters, who were at the top of the pecking order, often did not know the names of the men from the smaller papers, who were at the bottom. But they all fed off the same pool report, the same daily handout, the same speech by the candidate; the whole pack was isolated in the small mobile village. After a while, they began to believe the same rumors, subscribe to the same theories, and write the same stories.[58]

After Watergate, reporters returned to the practice of closely scrutinizing candidates' private vices. Moreover, with sophisticated communication technology, voters now have almost instant and saturating campaign information,complete with visuals, on television. Now the public laundering of personal weakness can end campaigns even before a single vote is cast. This public vetting of candidate weaknesses is more dangerous in the modern era. As Lichtenberg explains, "Even if a politicians character matters, it's not the only thing that matters. Yet the tendency for character questions to supplant others is very great. Sex in particular tends to distort public discussion by capturing people's undivided attention."[59]

The Transformation Of The Modern Press

While the presidential selection process has undergone a gradual evolution, the news media have experienced a dramatic and rapid revolution due to corporate takeovers and rapidly changing technologies. As Diamond observes, "The ABC, CBS, and NBC news organizations are now recasting themselves — not, as in the past, because of the imperative of journalism or technology or changing audience tastes, but because the networks new owners demand it."[60] Moreover scholars such as Bagdikian, Herman and Chomsky, decry "the alarming concentration in the control of information over the last half of the 20th century."[61] As Phillips states, "If the Industrial Revolution created a new elite and launched a new, business domination of politics, the knowledge revolution raises the prospect of dominant media influence — of mediacracy instead of aristocracy or democracy."[62] Parenti concludes that the media are not objective or honest in their portrayal of news. He also claims there is a relationship between ownership of the media and control of information. He says, "the top news executives are subject to the judgements of the ruling corporate directors and owners who exercise financial power over the organization and, if they so choose, final judgement over the news itself and over who is hired or fired at lower levels."[63] However, other scholars dispute Chomsky and Parenti on the point of corporate control of news and editorial content. For example, research by Fedler, Counts, and Stephens shows that chained-owned newspapers are not always homogeneous in their endorsement patterns. Chained-owned papers are no more likely than independently-owned papers in the same market to endorse the same candidate.[64]

Likewise, Diamond points out the central irony in this corporate transition. While former Soviet block nations continue to become more open and democratic, corporations in the United States continue to merge suggesting that "the oldest democracy" is moving toward "the same kind of blundering monoliths that the communist bloc has been fleeing."[65] Abramson, Arterton, and Orren further question the effects of the new modern media technologies on classical democratic theory, "Will the increased speed and immediacy of media transmissions provoke more and more specific demands on government, and a growing impatience with the slow, deliberative process of democratic decision making?"[66] As Diamond observes, with the addition of CNN in 1980, viewers have news on demand 24 hours a day. While the corporate buyouts of ABC, CBS, and NBC have resulted in staff cutbacks and bureau closings, "in ten years CNN staff has grown from 500 to over 2,000" and "CNN has opened news bureaus in Nairobi, Frankfurt, Paris, New Delhi, and Beijing."[67] As Schram observes, "This is a nation of nonstop news: morning news and noontime news and afternoon news and evening news and nighttime news and late night news and then early-morning news again."[68]

McWilliams suggests this instant news delivery has already manifested itself in presidential campaign coverage: "preoccupied with holding their audience, television programmers shun anything that might bore us — a logic that tends toward the lowest common public denominator."[69] Adatto notes that television news continues to shorten candidate "soundbites" while adding more interpretation of candidate statements and actions. Adatto discovered that the average amount of time on evening newscasts devoted to uninterrupted presidential candidate speech dropped from 42.3 seconds in 1968 to 9.8 seconds in 1988.[70] Jamieson comments that presidential candidates themselves have transformed their rhetoric into bumpersticker slogans in order to accommodate this shortened press coverage.[71] Likewise, Pomper explains that this new environment makes journalists lazy and less prone to cover important issues: "It permits them to be investigative without needing to know very much about complex political issues. It is much easier to grasp and convey the making of candidate images than to understand and explain the federal budget or national defense."[72]

Perhaps in an effort to gain more direct exposure or to avoid critical news analysis, presidential candidates are making more and more use of television talk shows and news magazines. Traditionally, public figures were questioned on Sunday news panels such as *Face the Nation, Meet the Press,* and *This Week with David Brinkley.* In recent years, there has been a proliferation of other formats, many modelled after CBS's *60 Minutes.* All three networks now have morning news programs: NBC's *Today,* ABC's *Good Morning America,* and CBS's *This Morning.* ABC currently runs *Nightline* after the late local news broadcasts and two other evening news magazines *20/20* and *PrimeTime Live.* NBC has added a similar program called *Dateline.* CBS also currently airs *48 Hours* in addition to *60 Minutes.* In an attempt to compete with CNN, NBC added *Nightside* and a cable news channel CNBC. Similarly, ABC added *World News Now,* as an overnight news service. PBS airs the *MacNeil/Lehrer News Hour* each weekday and *Washington Week in Review* on Fridays.

CNN, itself, has several news programs such as *CNN & Company, Inside Politics, Crossfire,* and *Larry King Live,* in addition to its 24 hour news service. The Fox network has several entertainment/news shows such as *A Current Affair* and the new *Front Page.* There are a growing number of syndicated talk shows airing at virtually every hour of the day in addition to traditional offerings such as *Donahue* and *Oprah Winfrey.* Moreover, these talk shows are becoming increasingly political. Seizing the trend, presidential candidates and political figures now regularly schedule themselves on late night television programs such as *The Tonight Show, The Late Show with David Letterman,* and *Arsenio Hall.* Perhaps Clinton can attribute part of his 1992 electoral success to his comfort with these new formats. As Marlette comments, "Clinton's political genius was in recognizing that a talk-show nation needed a host."[73] Even MTV, once an all music video format, added a news update and provided candidate forums during the 1992 campaign.

Political Ads And News Media Content

Another recent phenomenon is the merging of controlled and uncontrolled media during presidential campaigns. The paid political advertisements of candidates now make up a greater share of the stories on news broadcasts. A content analysis of television news coverage of presidential political advertising shows a steady increase in the number of stories from 1972 to 1988.[74] The authors of this study claim the increased coverage of political spots may be due to their ability to act as quick video for television journalists. This supports Diamond's research, mentioned earlier, into network cutbacks affecting the quality of news broadcasts. Similarly, the authors claim the increase in coverage "legitimizes" political spots as voter decision-making tools.

Ideally, we should expect the press to be neutral transmitters of campaign events and facts about the candidates. However, as we saw in the previous sections, the history of campaign journalism is over-wrought with examples of partisan press attacks. But there is a fundamental difference between press assaults and criticism from political opponents. We expect candidates to point out the flaws in political opponents during a campaign. But once again, modern marketing techniques and improved communications technologies raise questions as to the legitimacy of today's political advertising.

Again, the negativity in today's elections has roots in past campaigns. In fact, the history of paid political advertising is as ugly as the history of attack journalism. Negative and untruthful political advertising, like attack journalism, dates back to colonial times. Bennett states that James Madison publicly criticized George Washington for his questionable campaign practices involving the use of alcohol as an inducement for the support of voters during Washington's campaigns for the Virginia House of Burgess.[75] In the first contested presidential election between Jefferson and Adams, Republican flyers "pillared Adams as a monarchist."[76]

The campaign of 1828 provided the groundwork for hyperbolic political image-making when Jackson supporters borrowed a nickname given to him by his military troops in 1813 and created the "legend of Old Hickory." As Jamieson comments, "Although the enemies of earlier presidents had lampooned them with unflattering nicknames, Jackson was the first identified by an affectionate one."[77] The campaign of 1840, cited earlier in this report for brutal press attacks, is also noteworthy for further perfecting the image advertising technique complete with songs and slogans to promote William Henry Harrison's war record. That campaign was the origin for the familiar rallying cry, "Tippecanoe and Tyler Too."[78]

However, the onset of political parties changed the dynamic. For a short time, the candidates themselves did very little, relying on the political parties to do all the campaign promotion. As Jamieson recounts, "After being notified by a delegation that he was the party's nominee, the candidate typically delivered a speech of thanks and set about drafting a formal letter of acceptance that endorsed the planks of the platform on which the candidate would stand. After releasing the letter to the press, the candidate, with few exceptions, fell silent on political matters until notified of the election results."[79]

Skilled orator William Jennings Bryan changed tradition and made several speeches on his own in 1896. In that same election, William McKinley instituted the practice of directly responding to one's opponent by commenting on Bryan's speeches to the press from his front stoop.[80] The Wilson campaign in 1912 reinforced the right of candidates to actively campaign themselves by means of speeches and public appearances. Once that practice became generally acceptable, candidates and their staffs utilized any promotional medium possible, be it newspapers, radio, newsreels, or film.

Promotional techniques changed as new communication technologies emerged. KDKA, the first radio station in the United States, went on the air in 1920. At first, no direct advertising was permitted, but companies could use "trade-name" publicity and sponsor timeframes such as "The Maxwell House Hour."[81] Initially radio played host to political forums in which representatives of candidates discussed specific issue topics.[82] While radio stations provided news information and political speeches, commercial advertising "spots" did not appear until the 1930s. Television changed the equation even more dramatically. In the 1948 election, even with ample use of newspaper and radio, President Truman reported that he accumulated over 31,000 miles in 3 months in order to shake hands with approximately 500,000 voters. In 1952, Dwight Eisenhower was able to reach the same amount of voters in a matter of days by filming a question and answer program in a television studio and then broadcasting an edited version as a political spot.[83]

Diamond and Bates suggest that modern political advertising has had "systemic effects" on "the general strategy of campaigns, the overall styles of electoral politics, the kinds of candidates chosen, and the shifting sources of their support."[84] The results are costly campaigns, weakened parties, depressed voting participation, unsubstantiated attacks, mercenary political consultants, and a citizenry disconnected from its representatives. However, Jamieson and Birdsell suggest that, "In an information-poor environment filled with passive receivers of political information, ads perform an important function. The highest information gains produced by ads occur among low-interest voters."[85] Average voters do not gain much information from typical television news broadcasts and political advertisements actually provide more issue content. Moreover, Jamieson and Birdsell point out that radio and television have provided mass audiences with candidate debates and that voters do not have to depend solely on "spot ads and news snippets" in order to decide who should lead the nation.[86]

The Mass Media And Presidential Debates

The first nationally televised presidential debate was an intra-party discussion between Democrats Estes Kefauver and Adlai Stevenson in 1956. In 1960, Hubert Humphrey and John Kennedy held one televised primary debate in West Virginia. Kennedy and Nixon then held four televised general election debates which were widely heralded as helping Kennedy win in a very close election. In 1964 there were no televised debates either in the primary or in the general election. In 1968, Robert Kennedy and Eugene McCarthy engaged in a single primary debate in San Francisco, but no general election debate took place between Richard Nixon and Hubert Humphrey. In 1972, the Democrats held one debate at the University of New Hampshire followed by exchanges on *Face the Nation, Meet the Press,* and *Issues and Answers.* Nixon again refused to a general election debate.[87]

In 1976, there were several primary debates as well as three 90 minute general election debates between Carter and Ford. That same year, one presidential debate was held between Walter Mondale and Robert Dole. Once again in 1980, there were many intra-party primary debates, but this time there were only two general election debates. In the first debate, Independent John Anderson faced Ronald Reagan. In the second, Ronald Reagan faced Jimmy Carter. Similarly, there were two general election debates in 1984 where Walter Mondale faced Ronald Reagan and one vice presidential debate between Ferraro and Bush. In 1987, the two major parties formed a special commission to detail the format and sponsor future presidential debates. In 1988, we "witnessed the proliferation of debates with nearly triple the number of primary debates in 1984."[88] After hammering out an extensive memorandum of understanding with strict regulations on virtually every aspect of the debate, the Bush and Dukakis campaigns agreed to three general election debates and one vice presidential debate between Dan Quayle and Lloyd Bentson. In 1992, the Bush and Clinton campaigns also agreed to three general election debates and one vice presidential debate after public feuding and long negotiations.[89]

While political debate has been an important element in American elections since 1788, Jamieson and Birdsell explain that broadcast debates have both positives and negatives. They provide mass electorates with in-depth looks at presidential aspirants for an extensive period of time without advertising gimmicks and they force the candidates to clearly define their issue positions. However, "when candidates carry their own cases to the public through the forum of debates, clash is minimized and attempts to personalize arguments magnified. Here a speaker has much to lose or gain by voters' judgement, not simply of the case but of its presenter."[90] Furthermore, as we have seen, candidates may refuse to participate or engage in drawn out negotiations that result in formats that limit candidate exchanges and bear more resemblance to press conferences.

The Increased Pressure On The American Voter

American presidential selection has undergone dramatic changes since the framers of the Constitution encoded their version of the election mechanism for the chief executive. The system we have in place today now places most of the burden on individual voters both in the primary season and general election. Voters must sift through brief television news reports, slick political spots, and broadcast debates in order to select the American chief executive. Sometimes journalists act as a screening mechanism ferreting out candidates and leaving the voters with even fewer candidates from which to choose. Moreover, scholars have questioned whether or not the American voter is up to the challenge of the awesome task of rationally choosing the best candidate to lead the nation.

Recent studies by Owen and Popkin paint a more optimistic portrait of voter information processing in the modern communications age.[91]

Following Doris Graber's pioneering research in this field, Popkin suggests that voters do engage in rational decision-making during presidential elections. They may take information gathering short-cuts, but overall, given the proliferation of campaign information sources in today's society, voters still "tame the information tide quite well."[92] However, with the modern phenomenon of attack journalism, it remains to be seen if voters treat attack news items differently and apply different cognitive strategies to deal with such information.

The purpose of this study is to build upon voter information processing theory and to add to the body of scholarly studies that examine both the forces that create news content and the effect of media content. Since previous research has found that citizens are exposed to a plethora of news information and that voters usually have poor recall of specific campaign news items, this investigation addresses concerns that voters may react to attack journalism in a manner similar to the original magic bullet theory. As this research focuses primarily on the 1992 general election, the next chapter will consist of a description of the national political setting in 1992 as well as a brief synopsis of the entire 1992 campaign. It is my hope that this chronological sketch will help the reader understand the political climate of 1992. It may also be a useful reference source when incidents or events are discussed in later chapters.

Notes:

[1]Flanigan, William H. and Nancy H. Zingale, *Political Behavior of the American Electorate,* 7th edition, CQ Press, 1991:113.

[2]Germond, Jack W. and Jules Witcover, *Whose Broad Stripes and Bright Stars? The Trivial Pursuit of the Presidency in 1988,* 1st edition, Warner Books, 1989.

[3]See Sabato, Larry J. *Feeding Frenzy: How Attack Journalism Has Transformed American Politics,* The Free Press, 1991.

[4]Winebrenner, Hugh, *The Iowa Precinct Caucuses: The Making of a Media Event,* 1st edition, Iowa State University Press, 1987:3.

[5]See P. Lazarsfeld, B. Berelson, and H. Gaudet, *The People's Choice,* Duell, Sloan & Pearce, 1944 and B. Berelson, P. Lazarsfeld, and W. McPhee, *Voting,* University of Chicago Press, 1954.

[6]A. Campbell, P. Converse, W. Miller, and D. Stokes, *The American Voter*, Wiley, 1960.

[7]Key, V.O., Jr. *The Responsible Electorate*, Harvard University Press,1966:7.

[8]Flanigan, William H. and Nancy Zingale, *Political Behavior of the American Electorate*, 7th edition, CQ Press, 1991.

[9]Sunquist, James L. *Dynamics of the Party System: Alignment and Realignment of the Political Parties in the United States*, 1st edition, The Brookings Institution, 1973:13.

[10]Sunquist, James L. *Dynamics of the Party System*, 1st edition, The Brookings Institution, 1973:29.

[11]Phillips, Kevin P. *Media-cracy: American Parties and Politics in the Communications Age*, 1st edition, Doubleday and Company, 1975.

[12]Sunquist, James L. *Dynamics of the Party System*, 1st edition, The Brookings Institution, 1973:3.

[13]Phillips, Kevin P. *Media-cracy*, 1st edition, Doubleday and Company, 1975:3.

[14]See Phillips, Kevin P. *Media-cracy*, 1st edition, Doubleday and Company, 1975:132 and Black, Earl and Merle Black, *The Vital South*, 1st edition, Harvard University Press, 1992.

[15] See Ceasar, James *Reforming the Reforms: A Critical Analysis of the Presidential Selection Process*, Ballinger Publishing, 1st edition, 1982.

[16]Epstein, Leon, *Political Parties in the American Mold*, University of Wisconsin Press, 1st edition,1986:79

[17]Jamieson, Kathleen H. *Packaging the Presidency: A History and Criticism of Presidential Campaign Advertising*, Oxford University Press, 2nd edition, 1992:5.

[18]Euchner, Charles C. and John Anthony Maltese, *Selecting the President: From Washington to Bush*, 1st edition, CQ Press, 1992:114

[19]Ibid:183.

[20]Lowi, Theodore, *The Personal President*, 1st edition, Cornell University Press, 1985:86-87.

[21]See Wayne, Stephen J. *The Road to the White House 1992*, 1st edition, St Martin's Press,1992:13

[22]Ceasar, James W. *Presidential Selection: Theory and Development*, 1st edition, Princeton University Press, 1979:213

[23]Burns, James MacGregor, *The Power to Lead: The Crisis of the American Presidency*, 1st edition, Simon and Schuster, 1984:219.

[24]Epstein, Leon D. *Political Parities in the American Mold*, 1st edition, University of Wisconsin Press, 1986:88

[25]Salmore, Stephen A. and Barbara Salmore, *Candidates, Parties, and Campaigns: Electoral Politics in America*, 1st edition, CQ Press,1985:17-49

[26]Winebrener, Hugh, *The Iowa Precinct Caucuses: The Making of a Media Event*, 1st edition, Iowa State University Press, 1987:4.

[27]Schram, Martin, *The Great American Video Game: Presidential Politics in the Television Age,* 1st edition, William Morrow and Company, 1987:28.

[28]Pomper, Gerald M. *The Election of 1988: Reports and Interpretations,* 1st edition, Chatham House, 1989:4.

[29]Patterson, Thomas E. *The Mass Media Election,* 1st edition, Praeger Publishing, 1980:3.

[30]Gillespie, J. David, *Politics at the Periphery: Third Parties in Two Party America,* 1st edition, The University of South Carolina Press, 1993:1.

[31]Schattschneider,E. E. *Party Government,* 1st edition, Holt, Rinehart and Winston, 1942:1.

[32]Burns, James MacGregor, *The Power to Lead: The Crisis of the American Presidency,* 1st edition, Simon and Schuster, 1984:121..

[33]Dahl, Robert A. *A Preface to Democratic Theory,* 1st edition, University of Chicago Press, 1956:4

[34]Alger, Dean E. *The Media and Politics,* 1st edition, Prentice Hall, 1989:186.

[35]See Sorauf and Beck, *Party Politics in America,* 6th edition, HarperCollins,1988

[36]Burns, James MacGregor, *The Power to Lead,* Simon and Schuster, 1984:221.

[37]Phillips, Kevin P. *Media-cracy: American Parties and Politics in the Communications Age,* Doubleday and Company, 1st edition, 1975:168.

[38]Pomper, Gerald M. *The Election of 1988,* 1st edition, Chatham House, 1989:96

[39]Entman, Robert M. *Democracy Without Citizens: Media and the Decay of American Politics,* 1st edition, Oxford University Press, 1989:3.

[40]Graber, Doris A. *Processing the News: How People Tame the Information Tide,* 1st edition, Longman Press, 1988:xii.

[41]Lichtenberg, Judith "The Politics of Character and the Character of Journalism," Discussion Paper D-2, Barone Center for the Press, Politics and Public Policy, Harvard University, October, 1989:2.

[42]Jamieson, Kathleen H. and Karlyn Kohrs Campbell, *The Interplay of Influence,* 1st edition, Wadsworth Publishing, 1983:18.

[43]Barber, James David, *The Pulse of Politics: Electing Presidents in the Media Age,* 1st edition, W.W. Norton, 1980:313

[44]Hart, Roderick, *The Sound of Leadership,* 1st edition, University of Chicago Press, 1987:155

[45]Ibid

[46]See Sabato, Larry J. *Feeding Frenzy: How Attack Journalism Has Transformed American Politics,* 1st edition, The Free Press, 1991

[47]See Graber, Doris A. *Processing the News,* 1st edition, Longman, 1988:178-200, and Entman, Robert M. *Democracy Without Citizens,* 1st edition, Oxford University Press, 1989:77-79.

[48]Noelle-Newman, Elisabeth, *The Spiral of Silence: Public Opinion-Our Social Skin,* 1st edition, University of Chicago Press, 1984:148.

[49]Jamieson 1983:20.

[50]Freund, Charles Paul "Mud-Slinging is an American Tradition," in *The Quest For National Office*, 1st edition, St. Martin's Press, 1992:234.

[51]Wilson, Douglas, "Thomas Jefferson and the Character Issue," in *Atlantic Monthly*, vol. 270, no. 5, November 1992:58.

[52]Freund, Charles Paul, "Mudslinging is an American Tradition" in *The Quest for National Office*, 1st edition, St. Martin's Press, 1992:235

[53]Sabato, Larry J. *Feeding Frenzy*, 1st edition, The Free Press, 1991:25.

[54]Jamieson, Kathleen H. *Packaging the Presidency: A History and Criticism of Presidential Campaign Advertising*, 2nd edition, Oxford University Press, 1992:9.

[55]Crouse, Timothy, *The Boys on the Bus: Riding with the Campaign Press Corps*, 2nd edition, Random House, 1973:27.

[56]Ibid:36

[57]Sabato, Larry J. *Feeding Frenzy*, 1st edition, The Free Press, 1991: 25-26

[58]Crouse, Timothy, *The Boys on the Bus: Riding with the Campaign Press Corps*, 2nd edition, Random House, 1973:7.

[59]Lichtenberg, Judith "The Politics of Character and the Character of Journalism," Discussion Paper D-2, Barone Center for the Press, Politics, and Public Policy,Harvard University, October 1989:3

[60]Diamond, Edwin, *The Media Show: The Changing Face of the News 1985-1990*, 1st edition, MIT Press, 1991:11

[61]See Bagdikian, Ben H. *The Media Monopoly*, 1st edition, Beacon Press, 1990:223 and Herman, Edward S. and Noam Chomsky, *Manufacturing Consent: The Political Economy of the Mass Media*, 1st edition, Pantheon Books, 1988:1-35.

[62]Phillips, Kevin P. *Media-cracy: American Parties and Politics in the Communications Age*, 1st edition, Doubleday and Company, 1975.

[63]Parenti, Michael, *Inventing Reality: The Politics of the Mass Media*, 2nd edition, St. Martin's Press, 1993:34.

[64]Fedler, Fred, Tim Counts and Lowndes F. Stephens, "Newspaper Endorsements and Voter Behavior in the 1980 Presidential Election," *Newspaper Research Journal* 4, 1:3-12.

[65]Diamond, Edwin, *The Media Show*, 1st edition, MIT Press, 1991:xi

[66]Abramson, Jeffery B., Christopher Arterton, and Gary R. Orren, *The Electronic Commonwealth*, 1st edition, Basic Books, 1988:65.

[67]Diamond, Edwin *The Media Show*, 1st edition, MIT Press, 1991:55.

[68]Schram, Martin, *The Great American Video Game: Presidential Politics in the Television Age*, 1st edition, William Morrow and Company, 1987:27.

[69]Pomper, Gerald M. et al, *The Elections of 1988*, 1st edition, Chatham House, 1989:183

[70]Adatto, Kiku "The Incredible Shrinking Soundbite," In *The Quest for National Office*, 1st edition, St. Martins Press, 1992:248-253.

[71]Jamieson, Kathleen H. and David S. Birdswell, *Presidential Debates: The Challenge of Creating an Informed Electorate,* 1st edition, Oxford University Press, 1988:252

[72]Pomper, Gerald M. et al, *The Elections of 1988,* 1st edition, Chatham House, 1989:98

[73]Marlette, Doug "Never Trust a Weeping Man," *Esquire,* October 1993:71.

[74]Kaid, Lynda Lee et. al, "Television News and Presidential Campaigns: The Legitimization of Televised Political Advertising," *Social Science Quarterly,* vol. 74, no. 2, June 1993:274-285.

[75]Bennett, W. Lance, *The Governing Crisis: Media, Money and Marketing in American Elections,* 1st edition, St. Martin's Press, 1992:67.

[76]Jamieson, Kathleen H. *Packaging the Presidency,* 2nd edition, Oxford University Press, 1992:5.

[77]Ibid:6.

[78]Ibid :9

[79]Ibid:16

[80]Ibid:18

[81]Diamond, Edwin and Stephen Bates, *The Spot: The Rise of Political Advertising on Television,* 3rd edition, MIT Press, 1992:35.

[82]Jamieson, Kathleen H. and David S. Birdsell, *Presidential Debates,* 1st edition, Oxford University Press, 1988:88-90.

[83]Diamond, Edwin, and Stephen Bates, *The Spot,* 3rd edition, MIT Press, 1992:x

[84]Ibid:365.

[85]Jamieson, Kathleen H. and David S. Birdsell, *Presidential Debates,* 1st edition, Oxford University Press, 1988:125.

[86]Ibid:123.

[87]Hellweg, Susan A., Michael Pfau, and Steven R. Brydon, *Televised Presidential Debates: Advocacy in Contemporary America,* 1st edition, Praegar Publishing, 1992:2-4.

[88]Ibid;11

[89]See Chapter 2.

[90]Jamieson, Kathleen H. and David S. Birdsell, *Presidential Debates,* 1st edition, Oxford University Press, 1988:90.

[91]See Owen Diana *Media Messages in American Presidential Elections,* Greenwood Press, 1991 and Popkin, Samuel L. *The Reasoning Voter: Communication and Persuasion in Presidential Campaigns,* University of Chicago Press, 1991.

[92]Graber, Doris A. *Processing the News,* 1st edition, Longman 1988:201.

Chapter 2

Election Overview

As Gerald M. Pomper, author of a series of five books on contemporary presidential elections, freely admitted, he and his collaborators on *The Election of 1992* were "astounded" many times by the 1992 presidential contest.[1] Many "experts" believed that President Bush's re-election was inevitable given his dizzying approval ratings after the success of Operation Desert Storm. However, as early as a year before the nation voted, presidential scholar Everett Ladd recognized that two key opposing forces were at work on George Bush's efforts to maintain his job. First, support for the chief executive increases during significant foreign policy achievements. Second, presidential standing decreases when the economy is in recession.[2] Although he was not the one to wield the final blow, Democratic Senator Tom Harkin clearly recognized the implications of the second axiom in the fall of 1991 when he prophetically declared: "I'm here to tell you that George Herbert Walker Bush has feet of clay."[3]

By the fall of 1991, the gloss of the Gulf War could not conceal the rumblings of the American voter at home. As *Washington Post* staff writers Dan Balz and Richard Morin wrote: "Under indictment by an increasingly cynical public, the American political system stands trial a year before the 1992 elections, facing a crisis of confidence that rivals the period of disillusionment immediately after the Vietnam War and the Watergate scandal nearly two decades ago."[4] Moreover, this voter disillusionment began to manifest itself in tangible ways: According to *Washington Post-ABC News* polls, Bush's approval rating plummeted from 68% at the climax of the Persian Gulf War to 47% in late October, 1991; Democrat Harrison Wofford upset former Bush Attorney General Richard Thornburg in the Pennsylvania Senate race in early November 1991. Finally, two candidates, Patrick Buchanan and David Duke, emerged from Bush's own party forcing the president into a bruising re-nomination effort.[5]

The Challengers Emerge

However, even with indications of cracks in Bush's armor, the Democratic opposition was slow to form. As Aldrich explains, potential candidates weigh the costs of running for president verses the probability of winning. If the probability of winning is too low and the costs of running are too high, the candidate will decline to enter the race. Following this "candidate calculus" model, many of the nationally known names such as Jesse Jackson, Mario Cuomo, Richard Gephardt, Bill Bradley, and Jay Rockefeller declined to seek the White House in 1992[6]. Slowly a field of lesser known Democratic candidates picked up the baton. Former Massachusetts Senator Paul Tsongas was the first to declare his candidacy on March 10, 1991. The fifty-year-old Tsongas left the United States Senate in 1984, because of cancer and he claimed to enter the race against Bush as an obligation of his medical recovery in order to repair the damaged U.S. economy.

On September 2, 1991, former California Governor Jerry Brown announced an "insurgency" presidential campaign in a letter to supporters across the country. Brown, fifty-three, cancelled an expected run for an open United States Senate seat in California and immediately attempted to seize the moral high ground in the national contest by limiting contributions to $100 or less and setting up a 1-800 campaign number. Virginia Governor Douglas Wilder, a sixty-year-old grandson of slaves , coming off a historic victory in 1989 as the first African American elected governor of a state, also entered the fray on September 12, 1991. Wilder touted his tough fiscal policies in Virginia as a model for the nation. However, Wilder also became the first political casualty of the season when he dropped out of the campaign on January 8, 1992.

Iowa Senator Tom Harkin joined the competition for the Democratic nomination on September 15, 1991. The fifty-one year old Harkin used his fiery rhetoric and his working class roots to brand the president as out of step with everyday Americans. Likewise, on October 1, 1991, forty-eight year old Senator Bob Kerrey of Nebraska joined the field. Kerrey, a former Nebraska governor and a Vietnam veteran who received the Congressional Medal of Honor, attempted to strike a generational appeal in his opening campaign announcement. Moreover, in light of the Persian Gulf war, Kerrey's stellar military record was seen as an asset for Democratic challengers who are typically viewed as "soft on defense."

Finally, Governor Bill Clinton of Arkansas declared his candidacy on October 3, 1991. Clinton, a former Rhodes Scholar and a former Arkansas Attorney General, considered a presidential bid in 1988, but later decided he was not ready to compete at that time. That decision to bypass the 1988 campaign gave Clinton time to be the most "prepared" of the hastily formed 1992 Democratic field . Moreover, when Wilder dropped out of the race, Clinton became the only sitting governor in the field. This enhanced his appeal as a "Washington outsider" and a "different kind of Democrat."[7]

The Campaign Kicks Off

Unlike 1988, the Iowa caucus generated little national interest. As expected, native son Tom Harkin won handily capturing over 76% of the vote. The other Democratic candidates had already conceded the race to Harkin and spent very few days campaigning in the state. Campaign '92 seemed to unofficially kick off on February 18th, the date of the New Hampshire primary. Paul Tsongas became the surprise winner for the Democrats taking 35% of the vote. Bill Clinton, whose campaign had been plagued with charges of marital infidelity and draft-dodging, achieved second place with 26% of the vote. The other candidates Harkin, Kerrey, and Brown trailed badly with 11% or less and an organized write-in effort for Mario Cuomo netted only 3% of the vote.[8]

The survival of Clinton and the poor showing of the Cuomo write-in effort dampened talk of another Democratic "savior" jumping into the race. As Dan Balz and Thomas Edsall wrote at the time: "Clinton's showing in New Hampshire after three weeks of negative publicity over his personal life and draft record — and his campaign's skill in putting the second-place finish in the best possible light possible — provided a lift to his campaign. With an estimated 2 million dollars on hand, he will be able to compete in more places between now and the big round of primaries on March 10, Super Tuesday, than Tsongas."[9]

Unexpected Winners

In retrospect, the success of Tsongas and Clinton in New Hampshire, a recession plagued New England state, seems understandable. First, Tsongas, although relatively unknown nationally, lived near the New Hampshire boarder. His career as a Congressman and later as a United States Senator was well known to his neighbors in New Hampshire. Furthermore, he brought legions of supporters from nearby Massachusetts and he was able to form an impressive volunteer organization. Likewise, he developed a popular issue booklet entitled *A Call To Economic Arms: Forging A New American Mandate* which presented a blueprint to fix the ailing U.S. economy. At the time, Bill Clinton was the only other candidate to produce a similar document later retitled *Putting People First: A National Economic Strategy for America.*

As mentioned earlier, Clinton had nearly four years to prepare a first rate campaign organization. Like Tsongas, he exported hundreds of volunteers or "F.O.B.'s" (Friends of Bill) to New Hampshire from his home state. The mix of proper message and strong organization allowed both Tsongas and Clinton to prosper in the first primary. As David Broder commented; "Because they had thoughtful programs to offer, former senator Paul Tsongas of Massachusetts and Arkansas Gov. Bill Clinton, the two leaders, overcame obstacles that in most years would have doomed their bids. In other years, when real-world problems were not as weighty, Tsongas's mumbling platform style and his medical history would have made him the most implausible of presidential contenders. In most years, Clinton would have been scuttled by the personal stories that swirled around him in the final three weeks of this primary campaign."[10]

Clinton's Obstacles

It is important to examine the facts and circumstances of these "personal stories" that encumbered the Clinton campaign during the New Hampshire primary, because some of the charges would later haunt him in the general election campaign. Likewise, it is also important to note that both charges of womanizing and draft evasion had been recycled from past Arkansas gubernatorial campaigns. The marital infidelity story can be traced back to the fall of 1990 during Clinton's re-election campaign against Republican challenger Sheffield Nelson. Larry Nichols, a former Arkansas Development Finance Agency official, angry over his dismissal for long distance telephone abuse, initiated a legal action alleging that his termination was part of a cover-up of a government slush-fund used to finance Clinton's alleged extramarital liaisons. Nichols claimed to have tape recordings of the woman and he attempted to depose five of them including a Clinton staffer by the name of Gennifer Flowers.

Before Clinton's formal entry into the 1992 campaign, Democratic Party officials and several national news outlets investigated the charges from Nichols' law suit. Clinton denied the allegations. Many of the women identified by Nichols also refuted the stories. The issue seemed settled until a national tabloid, *The Star*, published the details of the legal action by Nichols. Then on January 23, 1992, the same tabloid published a front page interview with Flowers, who asserted that she had a 12 year affair with Clinton and that she had taped telephone conversations as evidence to support her claims. Perhaps sensing another Gary Hart drama, the national press began to pick up the story forcing Clinton and his wife to rebut the charges on a special segment of *60 Minutes* that aired right after the Super Bowl.[11] Clinton's aggressive gambit on America's top investigative news program, somewhat like Richard Nixon's 1952 televised "Checkers" speech, seemed to satisfy reporters and quiet the controversy.

Unfortunately, the quiescence for Bill Clinton did not last long. The Vietnam draft issue which unfurled on the heels of the Flower's story also had roots from past Arkansas gubernatorial campaigns. For example, on October 27, 1978, during Clinton's first campaign for governor, Billy Geren, a retired Air Force officer, accused Clinton in a press briefing of evading the draft by securing an ROTC deferment and then backing out of the commitment. After the 1978 campaign, the draft issue stayed dormant until *The Wall Street Journal* published interviews with former Arkansas ROTC officials three weeks before the 1992 New Hampshire primary. After questions from ABC News, the Clinton campaign released the text of a 1969 letter Clinton had written to Col. Eugene Holmes regarding the deferment. Once again, Clinton appeared on a special news broadcast, this time *Nightline* with Ted Koppel, in order to counter potentially career ending charges.[12] However, unlike the marital infidelity story, the draft dodging charges only temporarily receded. The story would periodically resurface for the remainder of the campaign.

Bush Drawn Into Battle

While Clinton scrambled for survival in New Hampshire, President Bush was unable to simply watch and wait in the Oval Office for his main Democratic opponent to emerge. He was drawn into a G.O.P.

primary battle by conservative columnist and television commentator Patrick Buchanan. Although Bush beat Buchanan 53 percent to 37 percent, the President's small victory margin sent the Bush campaign into turmoil. As Ann Devroy and John Yang observed: "Patrick J. Buchanan's strong showing in the New Hampshire primary has sent a jolt through the Bush establishment, which acknowledges that the president, who once anticipated easy renomination, faces a series of battles that could splinter the party, highlight his shortcomings and leave him a weakened candidate in the fall."[13]

Two days after the New Hampshire primary, another wild card emerged in the 1992 presidential sweepstakes. H. Ross Perot, the wealthy founder of Electronic Data Systems, announced on *Larry King Live* that he would run for president if supporters placed his name on all fifty state ballots. As Aldrich explains, most third-party challengers have little chance of winning the White House, because they are out of the "mainstream of political thought."[14] Likewise, Gillespie further explains that most third party candidates "lack the resources to purchase much access to the public via expensive newspaper, radio, and television advertising."[15]

However, the Perot effort was different from past third party campaigns. Perot could be construed as a political "insider" in the mainstream of American politics. He had been a contributor to many political candidates over the years. He had been active in the POW/MIA movement. Likewise, he headed a school reform task force in Texas in 1984. He also claimed to have foreign policy acumen having orchestrated the rescue of his company's employees during the Iran hostage crisis. Most importantly, his Horatio Alger like success from computer salesman to billionaire entrepreneur along with his plain speaking charm sparked an unusual independent national grassroots movement to draft him into the presidential race.[16] Moreover, he had almost unlimited personal resources to market his ideas and his candidacy by means of paid political advertising.

With the specter of Perot on the horizon and the dust of the New Hampshire primary settled, the race became one of survival for the lower tiered Democratic candidates. Jerry Brown hoped for success in the Maine caucuses set for February 23. The two sitting United States Senators, Kerrey and Harkin, set the South Dakota primary on February 25th as the final battle for political life. Meanwhile, the new frontrunners, Tsongas and Clinton, could target more states as the money began pouring into their campaign coffers after New Hampshire.

Tsongas selected the March 3rd Maryland primary to show strength outside his New England homebase. Clinton planned to win his first victory in Georgia on the same date and then follow with a victory in South Carolina on March 7th. These contests, they hoped, would act as a turnpike into the Super Tuesday primaries on March 10th. On the Republican side, Buchanan, like Clinton, was able to parlay his second place finish as an underdog triumph allowing him to carry on into other primary states. Moreover, David Duke began campaigning in Southern states hoping for regional success on Super Tuesday.[17]

The Field Thins

Jerry Brown narrowly defeated Paul Tsongas in the Maine caucuses on February 23rd. Brown received 30.3% of the vote to Tsongas' 29.0%.[18] Senator Kerrey picked up his first and only win in South Dakota on February 25th. However, this victory was only a temporary stay of execution for Kerrey. On March 3rd, "Junior Tuesday," both Kerrey and Harkin failed to win a single contest. Kerrey called a press conference in Washington on March 5th and withdrew from the race. Harkin also exited the race a couple of days later. For the remaining candidates, the March 3rd contests yielded mixed results. Brown chalked up another victory in Colorado with Clinton coming in a strong second. Tsongas scored wins in Utah and Maryland while Clinton won handily in Georgia.[19]

Any doubts as to who was the Democratic frontrunner were dispelled on March 10th, "Super Tuesday." Clinton amassed victories in Florida, Louisiana, Mississippi, Oklahoma, Tennessee, Texas, Hawaii and Missouri. Tsongas picked up only his home state of Massachusetts and two other small states — nearby Rhode Island and Delaware. Furthermore, Clinton showed muscle outside his home region on March 17th by winning Illinois and Michigan in the Midwest.

Two days later Tsongas suspended his campaign due to a lack of campaign funds leaving Jerry Brown as Clinton's only remaining rival. Brown staged a surprising victory in the Connecticut primary on March 24th and in the Vermont caucuses on March 31st. Brown's victories caused doubts about Clinton's electability in the general election. However, on April 7th, Clinton won the Kansas, Wisconsin, and New York contests, stopped Brown's momentum, and quieted his critics.[20]

The architects of "Super Tuesday" had hoped that holding several Southern primary contests on the same date would produce momentum for a more moderate nominee, who could go on to win both the nomination and the general election.[21] These primary schedule changes showed that Democratic Party leaders had finally acknowledged that the South was a "vital" region in presidential politics. As Black and Black argue, "Although the fact is not fully appreciated, the eleven states of the confederacy now constitute the largest region in the United States. Beginning in 1992, the South alone will contain 54% of the electoral votes needed to elect a president."[22]

In 1988, the Super Tuesday primaries did not yield the intended results of its Democratic architects. Although Senator Albert Gore amassed several victories in those primaries, Massachusetts Governor Mike Dukakis, the early frontrunner after the New Hampshire primary, was able to utilize his massive campaign fundraising advantage to remain competitive. Hence, Dukakis, a governor from the Northeast with a fairly liberal ideology remained the Democratic frontrunner. However, the 1992 version of Super Tuesday exceeded the intended result for the Democrats by producing a nominee with both roots in the region and a widely touted moderate ideology.

Despite the initial momentum for Buchanan after the first primary and the potential threat of David Duke in the South, the Republican primary contests after New Hampshire proved to be only minor nuisances for George Bush. The President defeated Buchanan in match after match holding him to approximately 30% of the vote or less. Duke performed even worse, dropping out of the race after an abysmal showing in his own home state of Louisiana. However, the Republican battles did expose areas of weakness in the Bush presidency. More importantly, the aura of invincibility in the Bush camp was completely shattered. Buchanan left Bush a wounded candidate for the general election.

The Primaries Upstaged

As Bush and Clinton continued to win contest after contest in May and June, amassing enough delegates for first ballot nomination victories, two events outside the presidential primary process captured the attention of the nation. First, a riot erupted in Los Angeles on April 29th when police officers were found innocent of police brutality in the arrest of Rodney King. By May 4th over 5,000 people had been arrested and the national guard had been sent in to restore order in South Central L.A.[23] The images of urban America in flames and feelings of racial injustice captured national attention and also provided fuel to the criticism that President Bush had allowed domestic problems to fester during his term of office.

Second, in early June, Ross Perot rocked the political establishment by announcing the appointment of two seasoned political operatives as bipartisan co-chairs of his campaign committee. Democrat Hamilton Jordan, who ran Jimmy Carter's successful 1976 campaign, joined Edward J. Rollins, a Republican political consultant, who helped engineer Ronald Reagan's victory in 1980. "At a joint news conference in Dallas, both Jordan and Rollins said they decided to break with politics as usual and join the Texas billionaire after concluding that neither party offered any hope of breaking the political gridlock in Washington or solving the nation's fundamental problems."[24]

The nontraditional presidential campaign of Ross Perot began to fundamentally reshape presidential campaign techniques. Eventually both Clinton and Bush begrudgingly followed Perot on talk shows such as *Larry King Live* and morning news magazines. Such formats had been deemed undignified in the past and had been mostly ignored by previous presidential candidates. Bush himself voiced frustration with these new modalities of campaigning: "I think we are just exactly where the heartbeat of America is. But you couldn't tell it because of all the noise and fury out there of Politics '92: endless polls, weird talk shows, crazy groups every Sunday telling you what you think."[25] Clinton, who had utilized televised town meetings early in the primaries, adapted better to the new forums. He later explored additional options such as MTV and *Arsenio Hall*. Clinton's decision to actively court the youth vote was also particularly significant as both *MTV* and the music industry had begun voter registration drives ("Choose or Loose" and "Rock the Vote") aimed at young voters.[26]

Likewise, Perot with his extensive personal wealth threatened to shake up traditional political advertising techniques. As one reporter remarked, "While Democratic presidential candidates have experimented with new ways of reaching voters, Perot could bring about a true revolution in political campaigning with an independent candidacy that is expected to make fuller use of available technology than anything seen in modern American politics with electronic town hall meetings, long blocks of television time, 'infomercials,' interactive 800 numbers and computers."[27] Furthermore, Democratic and Republican officials began to realize that Perot's new methods could not be ignored as many public opinion polls indicated that Americans considered Perot a legitimate challenger to both Clinton and Bush: "On the eve of the Democratic national convention that will formally ratify his nomination, Clinton finds himself in a deadlocked contest, according to a new *Washington Post*-ABC News poll. The survey found Bush was the choice of 33 percent of all registered voters questioned, while Clinton, who led narrowly in the last *Post-ABC* .poll, and Perot trailed with 30%."[28]

Clinton Bounces Back

Even though Clinton had overcome several controversies and had vanquished all of his Democratic primary opponents, the national fascination with Perot very nearly eclipsed his candidacy at the very time when it should have shown the brightest in the weeks preceding the Democratic convention in July. In addition, Clinton's smooth ability to bounce back from adversity during the primaries earned him the unflattering title of "Slick Willie." Clinton, himself, unwittingly encouraged this persona throughout the campaign by providing muddy explanations in the face of crisis. For example, before the New York primary, he confessed to reporters that he tried marijuana in college, but then he claimed he did not "inhale."

However, several savvy saving moves helped the Clinton campaign pierce the "media blackout" of his candidacy and refine his image. Clinton scheduled himself after primetime on the June 21st "Arsenio Hall Show" wearing sunglasses and playing an Elvis song on the saxophone. This became one of the most widely replayed television clips of the election. Similarly, in a more serious vane, while Bush and Perot took pot shots at one another, Clinton stayed above the fray unveiling serious policy proposals and filling in more details about his personal history on the talk show circuit.[29]

In addition, Clinton garnered significant attention by breaking traditional ticket-balancing rules and selecting Senator Al Gore, a fellow Southerner, as his running mate. As Quirk and Dalager point out, "It was ticket balancing of a subtle kind: Clinton's potential vulnerabilities as a foreign policy novice, prodevelopment governor, skirt chaser, and draft avoider were buttressed by Gore's Senate experience, environmentalist credentials, stable family life, and service in the Vietnam War. More important, however, Clinton's selection of

Gore satisfied the modern public concern that the vice president be ready and able to step into the presidency at a moment's notice, a concern born chiefly of the nuclear age, in which the harm an incompetent president can do could be cataclysmic."[30]

Finally, the Clinton camp utilized the Democratic convention as a mechanism to redefine the Arkansas governor to the American electorate. As Juan Williams noted before the convention media blitz, "The Democrats need a new candidate. At their convention this week they will try to construct one. Instead of backroom brawls and interest group squabbles, the New York convention will be about reinventing Bill Clinton; making the old candidate into a new, less-damaged and more interesting nominee."[31] By most accounts, the Democratic convention revitalized the Clinton candidacy and unified the party. Minor squabbles over the platform by Tsongas and Brown were handled smoothly. Governor Mario Cuomo was selected to place Clinton's name into nomination. In contrast to his sputtering address to the delegates in 1988, Clinton delivered a decent acceptance speech and the convention ended in song with a large gathering of unified Democrats hand in hand on the podium. The 1992 Democratic national convention seemed more like a scripted television variety show in contrast to the acrimonious political showdowns of the past. Clinton and Gore kept the momentum alive immediately after the convention by launching an extensive and widely covered bus tour around the country.

The Wild Card Folds

But, once again, Ross Perot nearly upstaged the climactic moment for Bill Clinton. The Perot campaign headquarters had begun to hemorrhage in the first few weeks of July. For example, Perot became increasingly testy with the press as reports continued to accumulate that he frequently used private investigators in his business dealings and in his personal life. Similarly, on July 11th, Perot used inappropriate language during a televised speech to the National Association for the Advancement of Colored People. A few days later on July 15th, Ed Rollins, his recently hired co-chair, abruptly quit after intense disagreements with Perot over campaign strategy. Then, in the midst of the Democratic convention, Perot held a news conference in which he declared that he would not be a candidate in the fall. At the time of this withdrawal, volunteers had collected enough signatures to ensure

Perot's place on 24 state ballots with another 7 states awaiting certification.[32] With Perot on the sidelines, the campaign temporarily reverted to the traditional head to head match-up. A two-way race is markedly different than a multi-candidate field. As Republican political consultant Doug Bailey explains, a three-way race changes the equation away from a zero-sum game. For example, an attack from candidate "A" might damage candidate "B," but it may also cause a backlash on "A" and benefit candidate "C."[33] Hence, without Perot, there was the potential for the remainder of the campaign to slip away from the issues and turn into a mudslinging contest. Up until his withdrawal, Perot's candidacy had helped to highlight President Bush's major weakness, a poor domestic economy. However, Perot was still able to focus the debate from the bench. "When Ross Perot took his dive, he left behind a tough deficit reduction plan, prepared by former Carter administration budget official John White," observed David Broder, "The Perot plan — like others of similar dimensions devised by less publicized people — now serves as a benchmark by which Bush's and Clinton's budget rhetoric can be measured."[34] .

Bush Continues Off Track

The month of August should have been one of the high points of the Bush campaign. With the Republican convention set for the middle of the month, it should have provided an opportunity for Bush to communicate his case for re-election and to rally his party solidly behind him. However, August proved to be a disaster for the G.O.P. Before the convention, *The New York Post* published a front page story alleging that the President had an affair with a former State Department staffer. The President was asked about the rumors in a tense interview on *Dateline NBC* Bush angrily rebuked Stone Phillips for inquiring about the matter in the Oval Office. Like the charges that hit Clinton earlier in the primaries, the Bush adultery story had been recycled from a previous campaign and injected into the 1992 campaign by a tabloid publication. The same story surfaced in 1988 and died off after the President's oldest son flatly denied the rumors in *Newsweek*.[35] But the Republican convention a week after the adultery flap provided no respite for Bush. In fairness, it was difficult for the G.O.P. to replicate the smooth atmosphere of the Democratic show. As veteran White House correspondent Mary McGrory observed at the time, "Their task is formidable. They must match the excitement and joy of the Democrats, and they don't have a great deal to work with: a panicked president, a vice president whose departure from the ticket appeals to 60 percent of the electorate, and a recession that won't quit."[36] In contrast to its Democratic counterpart, the Republican convention degenerated into a divisive affair outside the political mainstream. Speaker after speaker spewed shrill rhetoric attacking the Democrats without building a positive foundation for Bush: "In remarks not cleared by the Bush campaign, Pat Buchanan attacked Hillary Clinton as a radical feminist and accused her of likening marriage to slavery; television evangelist Pat Robertson denounced gay rights and complained the Democratic platform did not mention God; and Marilyn Quayle held herself up as a model for women because she had sacrificed a legal career for the sake of her family. Television commentary highlighted the strident conservatism of the convention."[37] Furthermore, Bush's nomination acceptance speech, though solid, did not match his stellar performance in 1988.

After the convention,once again, another event outside the political realm upstaged the Bush moment and dominated the news. Hurricane Andrew nearly destroyed South Florida and parts of Louisiana. While the President constructed an emergency aid package and vowed to rebuild the razed Homestead Air Force Base in Florida, the Bush campaign was again thrown off course by a domestic tragedy and unable to emphasize foreign policy accomplishments. In an effort to improve White House political operations and to shake-up his campaign, Bush recalled James Baker from the State Department and installed him as chief of staff. However, even with the vaunted Baker, the President's re-election seemed to be an uphill battle with a little over two months left to campaign. Moreover, many analysts viewed the Baker shuffle as an act of desperation by Bush.

The Media At Half-Time

At this point in the campaign, several studies of press coverage appeared assessing the 1992 contest at "half-time." Most media outlets had vowed to improve campaign coverage after the 1988 election. In reaction to criticisms, the major networks promised to expand candidate "soundbites" and to stick closer to the issues. Moreover, by the 1990 midterm elections, both print and broadcast media began checking the veracity and fairness of paid political spots aired by candidates.[38] But in spite of promises by the major networks to expand candidate "sound-bites," research on network coverage during the primaries by Ken Collier of the University of Kansas and Stuart Esrock of Bowling Green State University revealed that the length of sound bites in the 1992 primaries actually shrunk even further to an average of 7.55 seconds.[39]

Likewise, a survey of local and national press by the Times Mirror Center for The People & The Press at the conclusion of the primary season indicated that 57% of the correspondents themselves believed that barriers between the traditional media and the tabloid press had disappeared during the primary process allowing campaign coverage to highlight unimportant matters. Although 51% of local reporters felt that 1992 coverage was better than that of 1988 coverage, only 46% of the national press believed that coverage had improved. Furthermore, there was a sharp difference between the press community and the public at large on the issue of media influence during the primary process. Fifty-six percent of the press felt that the press exerted the "right amount" of influence, while 58% of the general public claimed the press had "too much" influence.[40]

Strategies For The Fall

Having survived the primary battles, Clinton refocused his organization and mapped out a unique strategy to achieve a majority of the electoral college in November. He made several staff changes. For example, James Carville was named undisputed chief strategist. George Stephanopoulos was moved from the travelling staff back to Little Rock as communications director. Mandy Grunwald was put in charge of the campaign's advertising strategy and Eli Segal was named campaign chief of staff. The new team decided to focus their resources on key battleground states such as Michigan, Missouri, Ohio, Pennsylvania, Georgia, and Louisiana. Little money was allocated to states such as California, Massachusetts, and New York where Clinton had sizeable leads. The team also decided to forgo spending in Texas, Florida, Mississippi, Alabama, and Arizona where Clinton had a chance to win, but the drain on precious resources might be high.[41]

While the Democrats retooled and plotted a strategy, Baker, Bush's newly installed political czar, seemed nearly invisible outside the White House and the Bush campaign team of Robert Teeter and Fred Malek remained unchanged. Vice President Quayle harshly complained that the

Bush campaign organization lacked both strategy and message.[42] In fact, Quayle's "family values" rhetoric seemed to be the only clear message that ever emanated from the Bush campaign. Quayle began this tactic back in May 1992 attacking the fictional television character "Murphy Brown" for mocking the role of fathers by opting to have a child out of wedlock.[43] Later, the Republican convention seized Quayle's theme, but pushed the rhetoric outside the mainstream.

While the Democrats and Republican geared up for the fall campaign, the Perot petition drive continued even without the candidate himself. State coordinators for Perot met with high powered delegations from both the Clinton and Bush campaigns who came seeking endorsements from the Perot volunteers. Furthermore, in early September, a bipartisan commission released its proposal for one vice presidential debate and three presidential debates falling sometime between September 22nd and October 15th. In keeping with other efforts to improve the 1992 contest, the commission argued for a new single moderator format with candidates questioning one another directly. Clinton accepted the proposal, but Bush rejected the plan. Making the most of this dispute, Clinton showed up at the site of the first scheduled debate in East Lansing, Michigan and attacked Bush for avoiding discussion of his record. The Clinton campaign further exploited this no-show by hiring individuals dressed in feathered "Chicken George" costumes to appear at Bush campaign events.

Perot Returns

Later in the month, Ross Perot began to contemplate re-entering the campaign complaining that both parties were ignoring the issues. Perhaps, sensing the damage from skipping debates, Bush reversed himself and challenged both Clinton and Perot to a series of debates with mixed formats.[44] Perot did re-join the campaign and all three candidates participated in three different types of debates. As Gillespie notes, the debate invitation to Perot and Stockdale was significant. Gillespie explains that "normally third-party or independent candidates can not beg their way onto the debate stage."[45]

The first debate on October 11th, followed the rules of past presidential debates with a moderator and a panel of reporters. The event was somewhat of a stalemate although Clinton scored points for reminding Bush that his father, United States Senator Prescott Bush, had stood against McCarthyism and that Bush should likewise refrain from attacks against Clinton's patriotism. Perot also drew praise for his folksy, straight-talking manner. The vice presidential debate followed on October 13th with a new format allowing a long segment of time with direct exchanges between the candidates. In contrast to 1988, Vice President Quayle provided a strong and spirited performance. Senator Gore defended Clinton in a cool, almost lawyer-like fashion. However, Admiral Stockdale, Perot's running mate, seemed out of place and many times yielded back his time to the other two candidates. This may have damaged any momentum Perot had built up from his own strong presentation in the first debate, raising questions as to how Perot could function if elected with an unprepared vice president.

The second presidential debate was held on October 15th in Richmond, Virginia. Carol Simpson of *ABC News* acted as an intermediary between the candidates and an audience of undecided voters. The personal attacks among the candidates ceased early in the debate after an audience member demanded that the participants, "focus on the issues and not the personalities and the mud." Bush and Perot were engaged and assertive throughout the night, but Clinton was clearly the most comfortable with this format, having held several similar televised "town meetings" during the primary season.[46]

The final debate on October 19th employed a mixed format with a single moderator followed by a panel of reporters. Bush again attempted to attack Clinton's character, but this time he was thwarted by Ross Perot who roundly criticized Bush administration actions supporting the military build-up in Iraq before the Gulf War. According to public opinion polls conducted before and after each debate, Bush did not "win" any of the debates. Voters picked either Clinton or Perot as the best performers in each debate with Perot improving the most overall by erasing the strong negative ratings he had accumulated before the exchanges.[47]

Clearly sensing the election slipping away, the Bush campaign (directionless after the Republican convention) finally settled on a strategy of attacking Clinton's character.[48]. In a move that would later cause her termination, Elizabeth Tamposi, assistant secretary of state for consular affairs, searched through Clinton's passport files for damaging information.[49] Bush himself, had attempted to raise the issue of Clinton's anti-war activities during the debates, but he was rebuffed each time. In the first debate Clinton directly admonished him about the tactic. In the second debate, an audience member stopped the attacks. In the third debate, Ross Perot stepped in and changed the subject.

The Ad Wars Begin

Having failed to engage Clinton directly on the character question, the Bush campaign took to the airwaves in a series of paid political advertisements in order to cut the Democrat's lead in the polls. The change in advertising strategy.seemed to reflect desperation in the Bush camp. Back in September 1992, the Bush campaign aired a five minute spot focusing on the economy in which voters were encouraged to call a toll free number for a copy of Bush's new "Agenda for American Renewal." Then in October, the Bush campaign aired an ad filled with scenes from Desert Storm and ending with a question of who voters should trust to sit in the Oval Office. At the start of the debates, the Bush campaign turned up the heat even more. First, by airing a spot in which the camera zoomed in on the cover of *Time* (which depicted a photo negative of Clinton's face) while an announcer accused Clinton of avoiding the truth. Then in the last weeks of October, the Bush camp aired a gloomy black and white spot featuring a vulture, implying that Arkansas was lying in ruins after Governor Clinton, and warning that Clinton would turn America into a wasteland.[50]

The Clinton campaign and the Democratic National Committee responded to the Bush barrage with quick response ads of their own. The Democrats claimed that they had learned from 1988 and they would not allow the Republicans to attack them in the future without rejoinder[51]. One spot interjected Bush's own statements with contradictory statistics. Another ad featured Bush's promises of prosperity at the end of his term and ended with an announcer asking if voters were indeed better off four years later. Moreover, both the Clinton and the Bush campaign began airing combative radio ads in key battleground states near the end of October.[52] The Clinton campaign also aired positive spots with footage from the Clinton/Gore bus trips and proclaimed a new generation of Democrats.had emerged.[53]

However, the most effective spots in 1992 were produced by the Perot campaign. While the Perot campaign aired several short spots focusing on issues such as the deficit and healthcare, millions of Americans tuned into Perot's lengthy "infomercials" in which the candidate sat at a desk and talked about the country's ills utilizing a plethora of charts and graphs.[54] There is evidence to suggest that the reason so many voters tuned into the Perot ads was because they were educational and generally positive. Daily focus groups conducted at UCLA during the campaign by Shanto Iyengar and surveys sponsored by the Times Mirror Center for The People & The Press indicated that voters were significantly "turned off" by negative ads in the 1992 campaign According to the survey, only 24% of the voters questioned rated Bush ads an "A" or "B" while 40% of the respondents rated Clinton ads "A" or "B."[55] Hence, the decision to turn to attack ads late in the campaign may have backfired on the Bush campaign.

Press Biased Toward Clinton?

In late October, with the airwaves saturated with political commercials, the news media began another round of self-assessment. This time the concern was whether or not the press was favoring Clinton during the final weeks of the campaign. In fact, the entire October 20, 1992 broadcast of *Nightline* concentrated on whether or not the press had already declared Clinton the winner of the election two weeks before voters had even gone to the polls. As Mickey Kaus of *The New Republic* commented, "Stories have set an unrelentingly positive tone about Clinton that contrasts sharply with the skeptical, adversarial stance toward Bush."[56] Seizing this criticism of the press, the Bush campaign began handing out bumper stickers instructing voters to "annoy the media and elect Bush."

Despite the early prediction by the pundits that the election was over, most major polls at the end of October showed the race actually tightened within the margin of error. For example, an *NBC/Wall Street Journal* poll had Clinton at 43%, Bush at 38%, and Perot at 11% with a error margin of five points. An *ABC* poll with a four point margin of error showed Clinton with 44%, Bush with 35%, and Perot with 16%. Likewise, a *Washington Post* poll projected Clinton at 44%, Bush at 34%, and Perot at 19% with a three point margin of error.[57] Moreover, the race was even more difficult to predict when the contest was viewed state by state through the lens of the electoral college. Although Clinton appeared to have a stronger base with solid leads in 18 states totalling 223 electoral votes compared to only 4 states solid for Bush totalling only 17 electoral votes.[58]

Election Day

On Tuesday, November 3, 1992 the election moved from the candidates, pollsters and pundits to the people. Millions of Americans travelled to the polls and cast their ballots reversing a thirty year decline in participation. Voter turnout increased to nearly 55%.[59] Bill Clinton amassed 43.2% of the popular vote and 370 electoral college votes. He defeated George Bush with 37.7% of the popular vote and 168 electoral votes. He also bested Ross Perot with 19.0% of the popular vote and no electoral votes.[60]. The Democratic party beat the 12 year Republican "lock" on the electoral college by wining 32 states. Clinton and Gore won solidly in the Northeast, the Midwest, the West coast and remained competitive in the South.

Clinton prevailed in most demographic categories taking some with huge margins. For example, Clinton received 48% of the women's vote, 80% of the Jewish vote, 84% of the African American vote, 61% of low income voters earning below $15,000 and 53% of voters over 60 years old. Bush only defeated Clinton among Protestant voters (43% to 38%), Asian voters (54% to 30%), and individuals earning over $75,000 (44% to 39%). Perot did not prevail in any category of voters; however, he did receive 29% of the Independent vote.[61]

Moreover, although unsuccessful, Perot received the highest percentage of votes for an independent candidate since Robert LaFollette achieved 16.6% in 1924. Other more recent third party challengers fared poorly in comparison to Perot's vote totals. For example, George Wallace received only 13.5% in 1968 and John Anderson pulled a slim 6.7% in 1980.[62] One can only speculate as to whether or not Perot would have accumulated even more votes if he had remained in the presidential contest throughout the summer. Likewise, whether or not the Perot coalition will remain stable and affect the 1996 contest, also remains to be seen. As Gillespie states, "it would be premature and risky now to proclaim that a golden third-party era is impending or likely. In national politics America's third parties historically have been either transient or obscure."[63] However, while many Perot supporters have organized into a public interest group called "United We Stand," Perot, himself, remains an enigmatic yet powerful force in American politics.

More importantly, beyond the man himself, the Perot phenomenon may signal another realignment in the electorate. According to Phillips, "Since the beginning of modern U.S. party politics in the eighteen thirties, emerging splinter-party tides have usually signalled the next major national regimes. The pattern — and it's surprisingly clear — seems to rest on the peculiar nature of the U.S. coalitions. Unhappy electoral streams shake progressively looser from the majority coalition, and as the predominant stream of discontent becomes clear, this movement foreshadows the realignment that will shape the next coalition."[64] With this in mind, Republicans and Democrats are already scrambling to find ways to lure Perot voters into their respective orbits for the 1994 midterm elections.

The 1992 general election also proved to be historic in terms of the turnover of membership and the demographic make-up of Congress. Voters elected 110 new members to the House of Representatives. There were 19 more women representatives, 13 more African American representatives, and 6 more Hispanic representatives. Twelve new United States Senators were elected in 1992. The number of women in the Senate tripled from 2 to 6. California voters picked two women for the Senate: Barbara Boxer and Diane Fienstein. Illinois voters selected an African American women, Carol Moseley-Braun and Washington voters supported Patty Murray. Likewise, Ben Nighthorse Campbell, an American Indian was elected to the Senate from Colorado.[65]

In South Carolina, the setting for this study, Bush won the popular vote with 48%, Clinton received 41% and Perot acquired 11%. According to exit polling by Voter Research and Surveys in New York, white voters won the state for Bush. Seventy-eight percent of the registered voters in the state of South Carolina are white. Bush received 60% of the white vote to 26% for Clinton, and 14% for Perot. Clinton received 91% of the African American vote in South Carolina. As political scientist Earl Black observed, "It shows that once again the problem for the Democrats is that they cannot get a large enough minority of whites to combine with overwhelming black support."[66] In the South as a whole, Bush also bested Clinton among white voters, but by a smaller margin 46% to 35% with Perot taking 19%. Clinton pulled 83% of the African American vote in the region.[67]

A Final Self-Critique By The Press

At the end of the election, the press once again engaged in a self critique. According to the Times Mirror Center for The People and The Press, eight in ten journalists rated the coverage of the 1992 campaign as excellent or good. However, 55% felt that George Bush was damaged by the media while only 11% felt that Clinton was hurt by the way the press covered his campaign. Thirty-six percent actually thought that the media helped Clinton win while only 3% thought the press helped Bush. The public at large was more critical of the press with more than one in three saying the press did only a fair or poor job during the campaign. Moreover, the press community gave general approval for new elements of campaign '92 such as talk shows and policing television advertisements. But the media was divided on press sponsored polls with 41% giving positive reviews, 36% negative reviews, 12% neutral responses, and 8% saying the polls had little effect.[68]

Now having examined the national political setting during the 1992 presidential campaign, the next chapter will focus on the local setting for this study, Columbia, South Carolina. Chapter 3 will also explain the panel selection methodology and the news media content analysis procedures. As mentioned earlier, it may be helpful for the reader to utilize the chronological election overview information contained in this section as a reference guide for later chapters. This may be particularly useful for the findings information in Chapter 4.

Notes:

[1]Pomper et al, *The Election of 1992*, Chatham House Publishers, 1993: vii.

[2]Ladd, Everett C. *The Ladd Report*, Fourth Edition, Volume 1, W.W. Norton and Co., 1991

[3]"Liberal Iowa Senator Becomes 3rd to Seek Presidency," *The State*, Sept. 16,1991.

[4]Balz, Dan and Richard Morin, "An Electorate Ready to Revolt," *Washington Post National Weekly*, Nov. 11-17, 1991:6.

[5]Devroy, Ann. "The White House in Disarray," *Washington Post National Weekly*, Nov. 25-Dec. 1, 1991:6-7.

[6]Aldrich, John H. *Before the Convention*, The University of Chicago Press, 1980:29.

[7]Candidate announcement dates taken from Ross K. Baker, "Sorting Out and Suiting Up: The Presidential Nominations," *The Election of 1992*, 1993: 42-44. Candidate biographies taken from "Democrats Who are at Campaign Crossroads," *USA Today*, September 13, 1991.

[8]Broder, David S., and Thomas B. Edsall, "Post-Mortem on New Hampshire," *Washington Post National Weekly*, Feb.24-Mar.1,1992:6.

[9]Balz, Dan and Thomas B. Edsall, "Heading South Where Things Heat Up," *Washington Post National Weekly*, Feb.24-Mar. 1, 1992:7.

[10]Broder, David S., "Bush's Problem Exposed," *Washington Post National Weekly,*Feb. 24 - Mar. 1, 1992:4.

[11]Maraniss, David and Bill McAllister, "Just When He Thought the Worst Was Behind Him," *Washington Post National Weekly*, Feb.24-Mar.1, 1992:13-14.

[12]Ibid

[13]Devroy, Ann and John E. Yang, "For Bush, A Quick Shove Into Plan B,"*Washington Post National Weekly,* Feb.24-Mar.1, 1992:8.

[14]Aldrich, John H. *Before the Convention,* The University of Chicago Press, 1980:24.

[15]Gillespie, J. David, *Politics at the Periphery: Third Parties in Two Party America,* The University of South Carolina Press, 1993:32.

[16]Mintz, John "Who is Ross Perot?,"*Washington Post National Weekly,* May 4-10, 1992:6-8.

[17]Broder, David and Thomas B. Edsall "Post-Mortem on New Hampshire," *Washington Post National Weekly,* Feb.24-Mar.1, 1992:6.

[18]*Congressional Quarterly Weekly Report,* July 4, 1992:70.

[19]Barilleaux, Ryan J. and Randall E. Adkins, "The Nominations: Process and Patterns,"*The Elections of 1992,* Congressional Quarterly Press, 1993:43-44.

[20]Ibid

[21]Norrander, Barbara *Super Tuesday: Regional Politics and Presidential Primaries,* University Press of Kentucky, 1992:27.

[22]Black, Earl and Merle Black, *The Vital South: How Presidents Are Elected,* Harvard University Press, 1992.

[23]Whitman, David "Beyond the Riot Epicenter," *U.S. News & World Report,* May 31, 1993:55

[24]Isikoff, Michael and Ann Devroy, "Two New Recruits Join the Cause: The Perot campaign gets a bipartisan boost,"*The Washington Post National Weekly* , June 8-14,1992:15

[25]Devroy, Ann, "Besieged, Battered & Bewildered," *The Washington Post National Weekly,* July 13-19:12.

[26]Cole, Kyle and Sonya Forte Duhé, "The Music Industry and Young Voters: The Impact of 'Rock the Vote' and 'Choose or Lose' on the Political Socialization of 18-24 year olds," Presented at Southwest Political Science Association annual meeting, New Orleans, Louisiana, March 17-20,1993.

[27]Balz, Dan "In Media Res: If You Can't Beat 'Em, Bypass 'Em," *Washington Post National Weekly,* May 25-31,1992:12.

[28]Balz, Dan "The Party is Betting Youth is the Ticket," *The Washington Post National Weekly,* July 13-19,1992:8.

[29]Baer, Susan "Slick Willie transformed into a strapping contender," *The State,* August 2, 1992:12A.

[30]Nelson, Michael "Conclusion: Some Things Old, Some Things New,"*The Elections of 1992,* CQ Press, 1993:190.

[31]Williams, Juan "Creating a New, Improved Clinton," *The Washington Post National Weekly,* July 13-19,1992:7.

[32]Cannon, Carl M. and Kristin Huckshorn, "Perot campaign unraveled behind closed doors," *The State,* Sunday, July 19,1992:5D.

[33]Bailey, Doug "The Third Wheel That May Help This Shebang Run Better,"*Washington Post National Weekly,* June 15-21, 1992:24.

[34]Broder, David "Holding Their Feet to the Deficit Fire," *Washington Post National Weekly,* August 3-9, 1992:4.

[35]Keen, Judy "Bush faces 'sleaze factor,'" *USA Today* August 12, 1992:1-2A.

[36]McGrory, Mary "GOP is in No Mood to Party,"*Washington Post National Weekly,* August 3-9,1992:25.

[37]Quirk, Paul J. and Jon K. Dalager, "The Election: A 'New Democrat,'"*The Elections of 1992,* CQ Press, 1993:69.

[38]Rosenstiel, Thomas B. "Media vow political coverage beyond soundbite," *The State,* Sunday, December 8, 1991:4D

[39]Collier, Ken and Stuart L. Esrock, "Who Gets What From the Networks? Network Coverage of the 1992 Presidential Primaries," Presented at Southwestern Social Science Association Meeting, New Orleans, Louisiana, March 17-20,1993.

[40]Kellermann, Donald S. "The Campaign and The Press at Halftime,"Supplement to the July/August 1992 issue of *Columbia Journalism Review.*

[41]Lauter, David "Clinton team outplanned GOP," Sunday, November 8,1992:4D.

[42]Dowd, Maureen "Bush's effort too little, too late," *The State,* Sunday, November 8, 1992:4D.

[43]Carter, Bill "Murphy Brown plans revenge on Quayle,"*The State,* July 21, 1992:5D.

[44]See Quirk, Paul J. and Jon K. Dalager "The Election: A 'New Democrat,'" *The Elections of 1992,* CQ Press, 1993: 71-73 and Arterton, F. Christopher, "Campaign '92: Strategies and Tactics," *The Election of 1992,*Chatham House Publishers, 1993:93-96.

[45]Gillespie, J. David, *Politics at the Periphery,* The University of South Carolina Press, 1993:37.

[46]Raum, Tom "Voters' questions fuel 2nd debate,"*The State,* October 16, 1992: 1A

[47]Quirk, Paul J. and Jon K. Dalager "The Election: A 'New Democrat,'" *The Elections of 1992,* CQ Press, 1993:73.

[48]Shogan, Robert "Bush plans new attack on character,"*The State,* October 19, 1993:1A.

[49]Green, Charles "Official fired after passport searches,"*The State,* November 11, 1992:11A

[50]Arterton, F. Christopher "Campaign '92: Strategies and Tactics," *The Election of 1992,* Chatham House Publishers, 1993:96-98.

[51]See Hershey, Marjorie Randon, "The Campaign and the Media," In *The Election of 1988,* Chatham House Publishers, 1989:73-102.

[52]"Air wars turn nasty with misleading attacks," *The State,* October 17, 1992:10A.

[53]"New Clinton ad to begin airing today," *The State,* August 31, 1992:3A.

[54]Quirk, Paul J. and Jon K. Dalager "The Election: A New Democrat,"*The Elections of 1992,* CQ Press, 1993: 71-75.

[55]Gunther, Marc "Voters turned off by negative ads," *The State,* October 21, 1993:9A.

[56]Kurtz, Howard "Are media smitten with Clinton?," *The State,* September 2, 1992:5A.

[57]Norman, Jim "Where those poll figures come from,"*USA Today,* October 30, 1992:4A

[58]Benedetto, Richard "Electorally a big lead for Clinton,"*USA Today,* October 30,1992:4A.

[59]Bledsoe, W. Craig, Instructor's Manual for *The Elections of 1992,* CQ Press, 1993:43

[60]*Congressional Quarterly Weekly Reports,* November 7, 1992:3549.

[61]"Exit polls: Who voted and what was important," *The State,* November 4, 1992:7A.

[62]Demick, Barbara and Robert A. Rankin "Perot supporters taking pride in making 'crazy' impact on race," *The State,* November 4, 1992:7A.

[63]Gillespie, J. David, *Politics at the Periphery,* The University of South Carolina Press, 1993:37.

[64]Phillips, Kevin P. *Media-cracy: American Parties and Politics in the Communications Age,* 1st edition, Doubleday and Company, 1975:138.

[65]Jacobson, Gary "Congress: Unusual Year, Unusual Election," *The Elections of 1992,* CQ Press, 1993:153-154.

[66]Scoppe, Cindi Ross. "White voters gave Bush his S.C. win," *The State,* November 6, 1993:1A

[67]Ibid

[68]Kohut, Andrew et al, "The Press and Campaign '92; A Self-Assessment," special supplement to the March/April 1993 issue of *Columbia Journalism Review*

Chapter 3

Data And Methods

In 1990, ShoeMaker and Reese issued a call for more scholarly studies that integrate media content and effects.[1] This research attempts to accomplish that goal by updating a panel study of voters during a presidential election conducted by Doris Graber in *Processing the News*. The methodology in this study allowed for a group of 18 voters and their voluminous news sources to be tracked over time during the 1992 presidential election.

This updated investigation attempts to determine how a panel of 1992 voters cope with the phenomenon of attack journalism. Sabato defines attack journalism as "the press coverage attending any political event or circumstance where a critical mass of journalists leap to cover the same embarrassing or scandalous subject and pursue it intensely, often excessively, and sometimes uncontrollably."[2] Since previous research has determined that voters typically have poor recall of specific campaign news items, this study addresses two key research questions: Do attack news items reach all voters regardless of political interest or media access? Does attack journalism affect individual vote choice?

In order to address these questions, the 18 panelists in this study were divided into four groups depending on their interest in politics and their access to the media: 1. High interest in politics/easy access to the media, 2. High interest in politics/difficult access to the media, 3. Low interest in politics/easy access to the media, 4. Low interest in politics/difficult access to the media. Separate interviews with each panelist were conducted every two weeks during the months of July, August, September, October, and November of 1992. Hence, based on the interview responses, we get both a long-term glimpse of voters in the decision-making process and an insight into how attack news items affect their vote choice. In other words, echoing V.O. Key, we can see if the voters "stand pat" with their early favorites or "switch" to another candidate later in the campaign.

The Research Setting

Graber selected her panel from a random sample of registered voters in Evanston, Illinois in 1976. My study employs the 1992 list of registered voters in the city of Columbia, South Carolina as a universe for the panel selection. Columbia is located near the geographic center of the state in Richland County and it is the capitol city of South Carolina. According to the 1990 census, Columbia is also the largest city in South Carolina with a population of 98,052.[3] As of 1990, Evanston, Illinois, the setting for Graber's research, had a population of 73,233.[4]

Like Evanston, Columbia has a major university located within its boarders. Evanston is home to Northwestern University, established in 1851. It has an enrollment of 14,198 students and 915 faculty members.[5] Columbia is home to the University of South Carolina, established in 1801. It has 26,133 students and 1,436 faculty member.[6] Similarly, as Graber was with Evanston, I am familiar with the print and electronic media in Columbia.

Table 3.1   Demographics of Columbia & Evanston vs. the U.S.

	Columbia	Evanston	United States
Median Age	30.4 years	31.3 years	32.9 years
Per capita Income	$8,986	$15,458	$12,287
Sex	48.6% male	48.2% male	49% male
	51.4% female	51.8% female	51% female
Whites	57.77%	74.52%	80.3%
African Americans	40.22%	21.44%	12.1%
Native Americans	0.19%	0.14%	0.8%
Asians	0.76%	2.72%	2.9%
Other Race	1.06%	1.18%	3.9%
Hispanics	2.19%	2.33%	9.0%

Sources: *City and County Data Book, South Carolina Statistical Abstract, World Almanac and Book of Facts 1993;* *Note persons of Hispanic origin may be of any race causing totals to exceed 100%

There may be advantages to updating the research by moving the study to a different region. According to the thesis of Earl and Merle Black, the South has become a "vital" region for electoral success in presidential politics.[7] Because of recent demographic shifts in population, unless a candidate is competitive in the South, he or she is unlikely to win the White House. Hence, the shift in setting from Evanston to a Southern city may actually enhance the research allowing for an in-depth examination of voters who seem to have abandoned the Democratic party at the national level in favor of Republican candidates.

According to Graham, from 1932 to 1960, the Democrats won all but the 1948 presidential vote in South Carolina. The exception in 1948 was due to South Carolina native son Strom Thurmond's Dixiecrat victory.[8]. The Republican party won its first presidential election in South Carolina in 1964, and the Republicans have carried the state in every presidential contest since then with the exception of the 1976 election when Jimmy Carter defeated Gerald Ford by 12 percentage points.[9] As Graham observes, "Only a significant turn down in the national economy could redirect Republican and independent support back to the Democrats. Even a fresh, moderate, or southern Democratic presidential candidate will be hard pressed to overcome the lasting effects of South Carolina's realignment with the national Republican party's White House design."[10] The 1992 general election provides both of Graham's criteria simultaneously, with a fresh, moderate, southern Democratic nominee facing an incumbent Republican president in a time of significant economic recession.

The Questionnaire

A questionnaire was created in order to provide a pool of applicants from which to select the panel. Graber based her early panel selection questionnaires on the election studies created by the Center for Political Studies at the University of Michigan. Likewise, I utilized the 1990 Michigan election study as a model for my initial questionnaire.[11] Questions focusing on levels of political interest and media access were printed on both sides of a legal size sheet of paper and mailed with a bright yellow colored cover letter and a stamped return address envelope to 500 Columbia voters on May 28, 1992. Research on postal questionnaires has shown that response rates increase with the use of cover letters, colored paper, consecutively numbered questions, and stamped return address envelopes.[12] The names of these voters were randomly drawn, with replacement from, the 1992 list of Columbia city voters provided by the Richland County Board of Voter Registration.

One hundred and thirty-eight questionnaires were completed and returned via the stamped, pre-addressed envelope that was enclosed with the mailing. The response rate was 27.6%. As Warwick and Lininger note, "Completion rates on many mail questionnaires are notoriously low."[13] Lavan explains possible reasons for this phenomenon: "People may have less incentive to respond when they do not have face-to-face encouragement," and "some may not understand the questionnaire."[14] However, Lavan also points out that questionnaires can be useful in the early stages of research.[15] Likewise, Bernick and Pratto state: "A compelling argument for the mail questionnaire is that a significant amount of information can be collected at a low cost. However, two disadvantages often cited in mail surveys are the potential for low response rate and response bias."[16] Although the response rate was typically low, (possibly due to the length of my survey) the problem of bias is somewhat negated since the primary purpose for the questionnaire in this study was to pre-screen respondents based on demographic data, political interest, and media consumption and to provide a pool of applicants for the panel. In that sense, the questionnaire succeeded.

Results Of The Questionnaire

Overall, as Table 3.2 demonstrates, the questionnaire respondents were close to national averages in terms of general attention to public affairs. Approximately half the respondents followed governmental affairs most of the time. Slightly more than 36% attended to public affairs some of the time and about 11% occasionally followed political matters . The returned questionnaires also showed that over 50% of the respondents held political discussions with family or friends at least three or four times a week. Furthermore, the respondents in this study had a significant level of interest in the 1992 election. Close to 88% were either very interested or somewhat interested in the 1992 presidential campaign. Over 80% of the respondents indicated that they cared personally about the outcome of the election.

Table 3.2 Degree to which respondents followed public affairs

South Carolina Questionnaire		Times Mirror Study of Americans
Most of the Time	50.7%	41%
Some of the Time	36.9%	35%
Only now and then	6.9%	15%
Hardly at all	4.3%	7%

Source: Ornstein, Norman, Andrew Kohut, and Larry McCarthy, *The People, the Press, &Politics: The Times Mirror Study of the American Electorate,*Addisson Wesley Publishing, Inc. 1988.

Table 3.3 Respondents interest levels in the 1992 campaign

Very Interested	48.5%
Somewhat Interested	39.8%
Not Much Interested	10.1%
Cared Personally About Election Outcome	80.4%
Did Not Care About Outcome	15.9%

Table 3.4 Degree of Political discussion with family or friends

Daily	14.4%
Three or Four Times a Week	36.2%
Once or Twice a Week	26.1%
Less Than Once a Week	18.1%

The questionnaire asked respondents to identify the positions held by Tom Foley, John Major, Yasser Arafat, and Alan Greenspan. This section of the questionnaire was later used in the panel selection process as a means to check the veracity of each respondent's political interest claims. For example, if a respondent reported that he or she followed public affairs most of the time, had daily political conversations with family or friends, and was very interested in the 1992 campaign, I expected that respondent to be able to correctly identify most of the political leaders listed and to know which party controlled Congress. As Table 3.5 shows, correct identifications declined significantly among respondents with lower levels of political interest.

Of all the respondents, over 50% correctly identified Tom Foley as Speaker of the House and John Major as British Prime Minister. However, less than half the respondents could identify Alan Greenspan as Chairman of the Federal Reserve. It seems somewhat unusual that more people (68%) could correctly identify Yasser Arafat than could describe other American political leaders; however, given the focus of this research, it seems ironic that the most controversial public figure is also the most readily identifiable by those who responded.

Table 3.5 *Correct identification of Political Leaders*

	Group 1	Group 2	Group 3	Group 4	All
Tom Foley	88%	53%	11%	.06%	51%
John Major	87%	54%	11%	0%	51%
Yasser Arafat	98%	92%	33%	13%	68%
Alan Greenspan	79%	47%	5%	0%	43%

Key: Group 1 [High Political Interest/Easy Media Access (n=64)]; Group 2 [High Political Interest/Difficult Media Access (n=13)]; Group 3 [Low Political Interest/Easy Media Access (n=46)]; Group 4 [Low Political Interest/Difficult Media Access (n=15)]; All respondents (n=138).

Respondents were also asked to name which party had the majority in each chamber of Congress. Of all respondents, over 77% knew that the Democrats had a majority in the House of Representatives and approximately 60% knew that the Democrats also had a majority in the United States Senate. As Table 3.6 shows, correct answers concerning party control of Congress again declined significantly among panelists with low political interest. As noted earlier, if a respondent claimed to have high interest in public affairs, but put down incorrect answers to the party control of Congress questions, that person was suspect as a potential panelist.

Table 3.6   Current Party Control of Congress

	Group 1	Group 2	Group 3	Group 4	All
G.O.P. House	0%	8%	15%	59%	13%
Democratic House	98%	92%	83%	38%	78%
G.O.P Senate	3%	14%	54%	53%	27%
Democratic Senate	97%	84%	17%	20%	61%

Key: Groupings are the same as in Table 3.5

Two sections of the questionnaire were designed to determine 1988 vote choices and the early candidate preferences of the panelists for the 1992 election. This information along with demographic factors was useful in ensuring that the panel was as balanced as possible. It is interesting to note that my questionnaire results concerning candidate preferences for 1992 seemed consistent with national polls at the time which also showed the race to be a virtual three-way tie. Approximately 28% of the respondents favored George Bush, 23% supported Bill Clinton, 23% selected Ross Perot, and 28% were undecided.

Table 3.7   1988 Presidential Election Vote

	Questionnaires	U.S. Vote
Bush	46.4%	53.89
Dukakis	35.5%	46.11
Did Not Vote	8.7%	N/A
Could Not Remember for Sure	0.7%	N/A
Marrou	0.7%	N/A

*source of U.S. figures: *CQ Weekly Report* 46 (November 12, 1988): 3245

Table 3.8　　Preferences for President in 1992

	Questionnaires	U.S.
Bush	28.3%	28%
Clinton	22.5%	24%
Perot	23.2%	33%
Undecided	28.3%	15%
Marrou	0.7%	N/A

*Questionnaire preferences as of May 29, 1992. Source of U.S. figures: CNN/*Time* poll May 1992.

Each respondent was asked a series of questions concerning their level of media access. These questions involved the frequency of both general news media consumption as well as attention to 1992 election stories. The Times Mirror Study of the American electorate estimates that 72% of Americans regularly or sometimes watch television news.[17] Likewise, over 70% of the respondents in this study claimed to watch television news at least three or four times a week. Over 81% paid at least some attention to 1992 presidential election news on television.

Table 3.9　Television News Consumption of the Respondents

Watched TV News Daily	42.0%
Watched 3 or 4 Times a Week	28.3%
Watched Once a Week	15.2%
Did Not Watch TV News	5.8%
Paid Much Attention to Election News Stories on TV	32.6%
Paid Some Attention to Election News Stories on TV	48.6%
Did Not Follow Election News Stories on TV	16.7%

As might be expected, over 91% of the respondents in this study said *The State* newspaper, based in Columbia, South Carolina, was their newspaper of choice. The daily newspaper consumption of the respondents in this study was somewhat less than the national average. Approximately 53% of the questionnaire respondents read the paper daily. The national average is 66% according to the Times Mirror study of the American electorate. Slightly over 73% of the respondents stated that they paid at least some attention to newspaper articles about the 1992 campaign.

Table 3.10 Newspaper Consumption of Questionnaire Respondents

Read Paper Daily	52.9%
Read Paper Six Times a Week	3.6%
Read Paper five Times a Week	5.1%
Read Paper Four Times a Week	7.2%
Read Paper Three Times a Week	5.1%
Read Paper Two Times a Week	7.2%
Read Paper Once a Week	10.1%
Do Not Read Newspaper	5.8%

*91.3% read *The State* newspaper

Table 3.11 Attention to Newspaper Articles About the '92 Election

Paid a great deal of attention	21.7%
Paid some attention	51.4%
Paid very little attention	15.9%
Ignored election articles	7.2%

The Times Mirror Study of the American electorate discovered that 52% of Americans regularly or sometimes listen to news on the radio.[18] Likewise, just over 52% of the respondents in this study reported that they listened to at least some campaign news stories on the radio. Slightly over 40% of the respondents paid at least some attention to articles about the campaign in magazines.

*Table 3.12 Attention to magazine and radio campaign
          stories*

Listened to a good many campaign discussions or speeches on radio	11.6%
Listened to several	23.9%
Listened to just one or two	17.4%
Did not hear anything on radio about the 1992 campaign	44.2%
Paid a great deal of attention to magazine campaign stories	10.9%
Paid some attention to magazine campaign stories	29.7%
Paid very little attention to magazine campaign stories	18.8%

Respondents were asked to indicate their age, sex, education, race, and employment status. As mentioned earlier, this information was useful in ensuring that the final panel was a demographically diverse as possible.

Table 3.13 Demographic Breakdown of Respondents

	South Carolina Questionnaire	Times Mirror Study of Americans
Male	49.3%	48%
Female	50.7%	50%
Age 18-25	7.2%	
Age 26-35	24.6%	
Age 36-45	29.7%	
Age 46-60	19.6%	
Over 60	18.1%	
White	73.9%	85%
African American	18.8%	13%
American Indian	1.4%	
Hispanic	0.7%	7%
Asian or Pacific Islander	0.7%	
Grade School Only	9.4%	24%
High School Diploma	17.4%	39%

South Carolina Questionnaire		Times Mirror Study of Americans
Associate's Degree	13.0%	19%
Bachelor's Degree	31.9%	18%
Master's Degree	9.4%	
Ph.D.	5.1%	
Law Degree	1.4%	
Employed	48.6%	
Retired	15.2%	
Full Time Students	10.9%	
Permanently Disabled	4.3%	
Unemployed	2.9%	
Temporarily Laid Off	1.4%	

Panel Selection

Like Fenno in *Homestyles,* an in-depth observation of 18 cases was the limit I could manage "intellectually, professionally, financially, and physically." The number of individuals interviewed may not provide "analytical range," but the intensive interviews and the extensive content analysis of each panelist's news sources do provide "analytical depth."[19]

Following Graber, I attempted to ensure a diverse panel by utilizing demographic factors such as age, sex, race, education, and occupation. With these factors in mind, from the pool of questionnaire respondents, 18 panelists were selected. The panel was evenly divided in terms of men and women with 9 males and 9 females. The balance between the number of men and women in the study is important, since Strate, Ford and Jankowski have identified a gender gap concerning women's consumption of print media. Women and men utilize television at equal rates to follow public affairs, but women do not follow the print media as much as men. Moreover, the use of print media advances political interest and participation more than the use of broadcast media.[20] At the time of the interviews, 10 panelists were married and 8 panelists were single. The age range of the panel was from 23 to 71 years of age.

This panel may have improved upon the Graber study in terms of its racial makeup. According to Graber, her panel "was not well balanced in terms of race."[21] Only two of her panelists were African American and both were women. My updated panel included four African American panelists — two men and two women. My panel also included a women of Hispanic decent. This is an important addition to the study, because as Earl and Merle Black explain: "Presidential elections still offer many ways to use racial themes to win votes... Prejudicial feelings and conflicts of interest between whites and blacks can still be exploited in elections, especially when the appeal can be packaged in symbols or issues that have no explicit connection with race."[22] Furthermore, as Graham explains South Carolina: "Political observers and street-level opinion attribute Republican ascendancy in presidential voting to the alienation of long-time Democrats by the positive civil rights position of the national Democratic party and the enactment of the Civil Rights Act and the Voting Rights Act."[23]

Like the Graber panel, the group in this study may be skewed in comparison to the general public in terms of higher education. five panelists had Master's degrees. five panelists had completed four year college programs. Three panelists had finished a junior college program. Four panelists had high school degrees and one panelist had a grade school education. According to U.S. Census data, as of 1991 only 21.4% of the U.S. population had four years of college or more.[24] The higher levels of education in both the Graber study and this panel may be attributed to the use of voter registration lists as a source for the panel selection. Moreover, this study attempts to draw conclusions in terms of media effects on voters, not simply the public at large. Likewise, Graber explains, "Education and interest affect the quality and sophistication of processing, but not its basic nature."[25]

The economic situation of voters is another important factor in vote choice.[26] Of all the panelists, seven claimed to be in comfortable economic straits. Six said they were in reasonable economic condition as long as no extraordinary expenses came into play. Four were economically marginal due to unemployment or temporary layoffs. One panelist was completely dependent upon public assistance.

In 1988, seven panelists voted for George Bush and seven supported Mike Dukakis. The other four panelists did not vote in the 1988 election. The returned questionnaires mailed out to the panelists on May 28, 1992 showed six panelists favoring Perot, five undecided, five supporting Bush, and two selecting Clinton.

The 18 panelists were categorized into four groups: 1. *High-interest in politics and easy access to media*, 2. *High-interest in politics, but difficult access to the media*. 3. *Low interest in politics and easy access to the media*. 4. *Low interest in politics and difficult access to the media*. Panelists were considered to be "high interest" if they indicated on their questionnaires that they followed public affairs most of the time, discussed politics regularly with family and friends, were very interested in the 1992 election, and correctly identified the political leaders and party control of Congress. Panelists were considered to be "low interest" if they followed public affairs rarely, discussed politics less than three times a week, and were not very interested in the 1992 election. Panelists were considered to have "easy access" to the media if they attended to multiple news sources at least three or four times a week and if they claimed to pay attention to news stories about the 1992 election. Panelists were considered to have "difficult access" to the media if they attended only one or two news sources less than three times a week, and if they claimed to pay little attention to news stories about the election.

News Content Analysis

In order to facilitate the comparison of panelist interview responses with their news sources, I conducted a content analysis of *The State* newspaper of Columbia, South Carolina from July 1st to November 3, 1992. The coding unit was the individual story. In total, 12,955 items were coded and placed into one of sixty four categories.[27] The categories selected were similar to the ones devised in the original Graber study with general headings consisting of campaign news, issues, arts, entertainment, and sports. Since panelists must sift through the entire paper for current events and campaign information, all items in the paper were coded including sports, business, and leisure stories. Items for newspapers were defined as including editorials, columns, features, and political cartoons. The daily comics section was recorded as one item. Excluded were advertisements, obituaries, puzzles, television listings and stock market listings. In addition, during the same time period, I tracked the local news broadcast of WIS-TV, the NBC affiliate, which broadcasts statewide throughout South Carolina. All panelists read *The State*, a Columbia based daily newspaper. WIS-TV news was the only local television broadcast watched by those panelists who followed local news. This is not unusual as WIS has been the dominant newscast in the Columbia market for a long period of time.

The panelists watched a variety of national news broadcasts; hence, I conducted a content analysis of each of the three major network news shows utilizing the Vanderbilt University Television News Summaries. Over 13,800 television stories were coded. Television items included all information conveyed during regularly scheduled newscasts, except advertisements. In the original Graber study, radio and magazine stories were not coded under the assumption that the information presented in those forums was very similar if not identical to the information presented on television or in the newspaper.[28] Moreover, I found, as did Graber, that during the interviews panelists rarely cited radio or magazine stories as the source of their information.

Interviews

A series of individual interviews, lasting approximately 45 minutes to an hour for each session, began in late July after the Democratic convention. It was my assumption that voters would begin to have a clear focus on the general election once the Democratic and Republican nominations were settled. However, the independent campaign of H. Ross Perot added an unusual twist to the research and may constitute a historical threat to the validity of my study. Nevertheless, I integrated Perot into the initial questionnaire and tracked panelist reaction to his candidacy as well as media coverage of his campaign throughout the general election.

Interviews were arranged in two week intervals on short notice in order to minimize any potential of special preparation or "studying" on behalf of the panelists. Panelists were reminded to maintain their normal routines and all were assured that their identities would remain confidential. The names cited in this report are fictional in order to ensure the privacy of the panelists. Since this research involved human subjects, an institutional review criteria form was completed and filed with the University of South Carolina's Government and International Studies Departmental Ethics Committee before the initial questionnaires were mailed and before any interviews were conducted.

Upon the permission of the panelists, interviews were tape recorded for accuracy. Interviews were arranged at panelists' homes, offices, or other mutually acceptable locations such as libraries or restaurants. If panelists were on vacation or away, interviews were conducted over the phone. In these instances, panelists also gave permission for the conversations to be tape recorded. Each panelist was assured there were no "right" or "wrong" responses during the conversations. The initial questionnaire as well as the follow-up interview questions were based on selected questions from the 1990 University of Michigan's National Election Study. The interviews were "moderately scheduled" with broad, open-ended questions concerning each panelist's reaction to the presidential campaign and media coverage of the election.[29] Some questions were presented as "story-telling" exercises such as "If your friends were away on vacation, and if they wanted to know what was going on in the presidential election when they returned, what would you tell them?" Open-ended questions are effective instruments in face-to-face encounters and they allowed for the interviews to proceed more like conversations similar to day-to-day political discussions with family or friends. This lowered the threat of a testing effect.

Even with the aforementioned safeguards, there is a potential that the interview process itself may have sensitized the panelists to the 1992 campaign, contributing to a more attentive audience than would otherwise be the case.[30] This may be particularly true in the cases of panelists with low political interest and easy media access. However, panelists in that group did not appear to significantly alter their news media consumption of the election throughout the interview process. Moreover, their general disinterest or disregard for the political process seemed to remain consistent from the start of the interviews to the finish of the interview process.

As mentioned earlier, this study updates the Graber research and pays special attention to the new "attack journalism." My research addresses concerns that attack news items may provide a magic bullet effect on voters. I expect that attack journalism will reach all panelists equally regardless of political interest or media access. Moreover, I expect that such news items will affect individual vote choice. To test these hypotheses, I will match interview responses with news content and then compare the responses of each of the four groups: High political interest/easy media access, High political interest/difficult media access, Low political interest/easy media access, and Low political interest/difficult media access. Moreover, I will track whether or not the panelists stick with their early candidate favorites or switch before they cast their ballots and I will attempt to determine whether or not media influences affected candidate support.

Panelist Sketches

Table 3.14 High-interest, Easy access group

Name (fictional)	Age	Race/Sex	Education	Occupation
Carl Adams	36	WM	College	Accountant
Ron Burton	40	WM	College	Unemployed
Bill Creighton	44	BM	Junior College	Construction
Pete Diedrich	62	BM	Master's	Government
Leon Evans	71	WM	Junior College	Retired

Carl Adams, 36, married, college graduate, currently working as an accountant. He follows public affairs most of the time and is very interested in the presidential campaign this year. He watches television news daily and pays close attention to programs about the election. He also reads *The State* daily, again giving close scrutiny to articles about the campaign. Carl follows radio news programs covering the election and keeps up with news magazines. In 1988, he voted for George Bush, and he expects to do so again in 1992.

In his initial interview on July 19, 1992, Carl said, "I'm mainly a Republican, but I will voted for a good Democrat." When asked to define a political party, he commented: "You align yourself with a political party that has the same general philosophy that you do. Or you may not align yourself with a party. You may vote for each individual person who has the same philosophy you do. Being here in the South, this used to be a Democratic stronghold for years and years and years, but the Democrats have shifted from their original philosophy. And the Republicans have taken that over. The philosophy's the same. It's just that the parties have switched."

Carl said the main problem facing the country "is obviously the economy. That's the major problem right now. I don't think there's much more to worry about national security, of course, with the demise of the communist situation. So the focus has to be put back onto the economy, especially dealing with your major competitors — Japan and Germany, and this type deal." When asked which news source he would first turn to during a major news event, he responded, "Well, obviously the TV set. I read the paper everyday, but the local paper's sort of not very in-depth. In fact your really don't get very much information anywhere." He said, "I'm a flipper; I switch stations. If there's an article I don't like, I just flip it — not giving any preference to any station. *MacNeil/Leher,* I think, is a little bit better than most, but they're so dry and boring."

Ronald Burton, 40, is a married college graduate currently unemployed, but signed up with a temporary agency for potential work assignments. He spends free time at the library and is an avid follower of public affairs. He is very interested in the campaign this year and he says he talks about it with family or friends about three or four times a week. He watches television news daily and closely monitors programs about the presidential election. He reads several newspapers including *The State, The Wall Street Journal,* and *The New York Times.* He follows some radio coverage of the campaign and reads a great deal about the race in news magazines. In 1988, he voted for Governor Dukakis, and in his initial questionnaire he favored Ross Perot.

In his initial interview on July 19, 1992, Ronald said, "a political party is a group of people interested in helping themselves — economically, financially — to benefit themselves through connections with those in office or to help themselves get elected to office." He considered himself to be an Independent voter. When asked to cite the most important problem facing the country, he said, "I think the economy is the most important problem. We got maybe 20 million people unemployed, 25 million under-employed, the next 60 million or so in a position of correct employment, but we've been steadily losing ground for about 18 years, coming up on 20 years now. I think the economy, if we could turn around our economic ways, we could solve a lot of the inner city problems and a lot of the, ah, social problems. I see by putting people back to work and giving them with dignity, the pride of having a job and a decent place to stay, they'll be able to afford that stuff. Not government handouts and public housing." When asked where he would seek information during a major news event, he said, "I suppose it would be television." He said he trusted ABC the most, because "of the three anchors, I prefer Peter Jennings. I think they do try to present the news a little more fairly. All of them attack. All of them defend. But I just prefer him over Brokaw or, ah, Rather. I think he's a little more intelligent or he tries to be more impartial."

Bill Creighton, 44, is a married carpenter who has been temporarily laid off from his construction company due to the recession. He discusses politics with his family and friends everyday and he follows governmental affairs most of the time. He watches television news and reads *The State* daily, but he pays only some attention to news paper accounts about the 1992 campaign. He closely follows radio coverage of the election, but he reads very little about the campaign in news magazines. In 1988, he voted for Governor Dukakis, and in his initial questionnaire he selected Ross Perot.

In his initial interview on July 22, 1992, Mr Creighton considered himself to be an independent voter. He said, "I think a lot of folks have a tendency to vote party line. Because you have, instead of doing what's supposed to be done, you have people voting on party lines and not representing the people. It would be nice if we didn't have a two party system, but the Democrats and the Republicans say that the stability of our country has been assured for over 200 years through the two party system or three party system. Oh well, that has a little bit of credence, but it has to get back down to representing the people. We get away from what we need to be talking about. We need to be talking about issues. To get any real recognition and any funding, if you go in as a Democrat, you'll get funding from the party. If you go Republican, it is the very same thing. But an Independent, all your financial support is just that way, independent. So its just a little bit easier to get your point across through the electronic media if you belong to a party."

Mr. Creighton said he trusted CNN the most. He said, "All throughout the Desert Storm Operation I was fixed to CNN day and night. Not because of my fascination with the TV, but because of my fascination with this was the first time we've ever seen a war live. It was just fascinating. To hear a person talk about the danger of a certain situation and then the very next minute be exposed to that danger. To see the panic, the electronic media has really done a lot to see the horror." When asked to cite the most important problem facing the country, he said, "Of all the problems, even the racial problems, I really do think that unless we get our economic house in order, we're in for really rough days. I think that's number one right now."

Pete Diedrich, 62, is a married government executive with a Master's degree plus some additional graduate credit hours. He also is very proud to be an honorably discharged Korean War veteran. He is very much interested in the 1992 election and he talks about politics everyday with family or friends. He watches television news everyday and he closely monitors programs about the campaign. He reads several newspapers including *The State, Black News,* and *The Charlotte Observer.* He also closely follows the election on radio and in news magazines. In 1988, he voted for Governor Dukakis, and he is a strong supporter of Bill Clinton in 1992.

In his initial interview on July 20, 1994, Mr. Diedrich considered himself to be a strong Democrat. He said, "I have no doubt the Republicans may be well-intentioned, but they just don't get it. Unless you are middle class or upper, middle class, they don't even know you exist." When asked to identify the most critical issues facing the country, he said, "the most important problem we have in America is health and education. In a democracy, a democracy is predicated — when our forefathers put together our constitution, they assumed that Americans were going to be literate and were going to be healthy. Democracy can't work, if I — if somebody said to me, 'if you only had so much money in America, where would you put the money?' I'd put the money into health and education." When asked which news source he trusted the most, he said, "I trust Dan Rather and CBS much more than NBC or ABC. When I look at the way people report and the spin that they put on it, I'm not saying I just trust CBS. I trust Dan Rather. In the mornings I like Byrant Gumble, but in the evenings I watch Dan Rather. But I think those are reliable. What's this guy on at night, Rush, ah, Limbaugh. I think he ought to be taken off. He is so slanted and biased, it's a shame."

Leon Evans, 71, is a retired public accountant. He is married and he holds an associates degree in business. He closely scrutinizes government and public affairs and he is very interested in the 1992 presidential campaign. He discusses politics everyday with either family or friends and he watches several programs about the election each day. He is an avid reader of *The State* and he pays a great deal of attention to news articles about the campaign . He frequently contacts public officials and agencies in order to research political issues, but he does not follow the election on radio or in news magazines. In 1988, he voted for Governor Dukakis, but in his initial questionnaire, he was undecided about the 1992 race.

In his initial interview on July 23, 1992, Leon said that he had "no party identification and no religious preferences." When asked what were the most important problems facing the country, he responded: "The main problem is to get industry back in the country. We need to retool and get jobs back. We need to get money back into the hands of people that can buy things. You know it takes six people to make one product a person needs. We're a service nation now, not a manufacturing country. Money is like blood and we're hemorrhaging as a country. We're operating on borrowed Japanese money." Leon says he trusts CNN the most as a news source, but "if you want to go into detail, you've got to check the newspaper."

Table 3.15 High-interest, Difficult access group

Name (fictional)	Age	Race/Sex	Education	Occupation
Carol Bach	37	WF	Master's	Teacher
Marc Jackman	38	WM	Master's	Government
Charles Ippolitos	40	WM	College	Accountant
Maggie Gaylord	43	BF	Junior College	Nurse
Hilda Holmquist	54	WF	Master's	Government

Carol Bach, 37, single, a high school teacher with a Master's of Arts in Teaching. She is well informed on public affairs and she discusses political issues daily with family or friends. She holds a second job and has a very busy schedule; hence, she only watches television news occasionally. She reads either *The State* or *The Greenville News & Courier* about twice a week and she does not follow the campaign on radio. She does periodically read about the election in *Newsweek*. In 1988, she voted for Governor Dukakis, and in her initial questionnaire she expressed a preference for Ross Perot.

In her initial interview on July 23, 1992, Carol defined a political party as "a power factory" and she characterized herself as an independent. When asked what were the most important problems facing the country, she said: "The economy and homelessness. The economy and the cost of healthcare. The economy and job loss." Although she follows NBC news regularly, she was unable to cite a specific news source which she trusts the most. When asked what source she would turn to if an important news event were taking place, she responded, "That depends — the written word usually."

Marc Jackman, 38, married, a government administrator with a Master's degree. He follows public affairs most of the time and is very interested in the 1992 presidential campaign. He discusses politics with family or friends three or four times a week. He does not watch much television news and he does not follow programs about the election. He does not read *The State* very often, but he occasionally listens to speeches or discussions about the campaign on his car radio. He rarely reads about the election in news magazines. His sporadic media access is due to a demanding workload and family obligations. In 1988, he voted for George Bush, and in his initial questionnaire, he favored Ross Perot.

During his initial interview on July 20, 1992, he said, "I consider myself an Independent. I do not fully relate to either of the major parties." When asked what were the most important problems facing the country he responded: "The most important problems facing America are the economy, healthcare, and the national debt. In a nation as wealthy as the U.S., it's a shame that we lose so many jobs to foreign competitors — that so many Americans, especially older Americans, do not receive adequate healthcare, and that we owe so much money. I think government spends too much money in the wrong places. The largest problems, in my view, is that government is run by special interests. That's why the economy and healthcare is in its current state." The news source he trusts the most is CNN, because, "They seem to be news specialists and their coverage is better or more complete. CNN runs 24 hours every day and they constantly update their stories."

Charles Ippolitos, 40, single, an account manager with a college degree. He is currently very interested in the presidential campaign and he follows public affairs most of the time. He cares deeply about the outcome of the election, but he only discusses politics with family or friends once or twice a week. He only manages to watch television news once a week and he occasionally watches a program about the campaign. Most days he scans *The State* or *The Wall Street Journal;* however, he says he usually skips stories about the election. In 1988, he voted for George Bush and in his initial questionnaire he selected Ross Perot.

During his initial interview on July 22, 1993, Charles did not identify himself with either party. He said, "Political parties are not as relevant as they once were. They shift from one side of the spectrum to the other. Like my father used to say, 'I never voted for a party, but for a person to do the best job.' Up until now, I was a Republican. Now I'm an independent, but I'm disappointed with Perot." When asked to identify the most important problems facing the country, he cited the "level of jobs, number of layoffs, and abortion, an emotional issue presidential candidates don't need to be running on." The most important problem to him was "the lack of jobs." The news source he trusts the most is "TV reporting — I like the A.B.C. organization, because of the personalities there and *Nightline.*"

Maggie Gaylord, 43, a single mother with an associates degree in nursing. She discusses politics with family and friends three or four times a week and she is very interested in the presidential election this year. She watches television news three times a week, but she says she pays little attention to stories and programs about the campaign. She does not read any news magazines and she looks at *The State* about once a week. In 1988, Maggie voted for Dukakis, but she indicated in her initial questionnaire that she was undecided about who to support in the 1992 contest.

In her initial interview on July 21, 1993, Maggie said she did not consider herself a member of a political party. She said, "I usually split my ticket." When asked to identify the major problems facing the country, she said: "Now that's a pretty hard question. Well, yes, O.K. Like, you know, we do have homeless people, living in a box, sleeping in boxes. Russia and Poland and countries like that are going through their problems. I'm not the type of person who can't see beyond the boundaries of the United States, uh, and I think that, uh, the American people or the American public and the politicians are as prejudice or worse as they've ever been. I think the last time we had a decent president was from Kennedy back and we have not had a decent presidency since. I feel like the last thirty years with, uh, human rights and, you know, racial things are probably slipped under the rug and not dealt with. You know people of color and females. That's my general feeling."

When asked what was the news source she most trusted, Maggie said CNN due to their coverage of the Desert Storm crisis. She said she had a relative who served in the operation and that CNN was the only station which gave her updates "every five minutes."

Hilda Holmquist, 54, single, a self-proclaimed "government bureaucrat" working in a state agency. She follows public affairs most of the time and she discusses politics with family and friends three or four times a week. She watches television news three or four times a week, but she claims to ignore campaign stories because they are "98% bull." She tries to read *The State* most days, but she says she skips stories about the election. She does not follow the campaign on the radio or in news magazines. In 1988, she voted for Mike Dukakis, but she was undecided on the 1992 race according to her initial questionnaire.

Although she did write on her form that "Perot is an unknown factor for me and I would have preferred Cuomo."

In her initial interview on July 19, 1994, Hilda said that it was easy to see that she was a Democrat. However, she claimed that political parties "don't have a lot of relevance in 1992. In the sense that, historically, I've always thought of the Democrats as being, ah, supportive of the blue collar worker, supportive of social health programs, supportive of kind of the Great Society stuff. I've thought of the Republicans as being entirely hooked into business and being very capitalist and very supportive of big business and money and a kind of 'let them eat cake philosophy' about others." She said the most important problems facing America are "the national deficit, the loss of manufacturing jobs, a healthcare system that is out of control, and education. I think success in anything that we do from now on is going to be predicated on getting control of the national debt. I think we are mortgaging ourselves out of existence." She said she trusted "CNN, because they are going to be the first ones there and you're going to see in the raw what's going on before the commentators get a chance to tell you what you're seeing. They give you a greater opportunity to make your own judgement about what's going on initially."

Table 3.16 Low-interest, easy access group

Name (fictional)	Age	Race/Sex	Education	Occupation
Penny Lobmon	23	WF	College	Computer Support
Craig Koll	26	WM	High School	Receiving Clerk
Elaine Miller	41	WF	High School	Marketing Arts
William Nystrum	45	WM	Master's	Programmer

Penny Lobmon, 23, single, a recent college graduate who has had difficulty finding permanent employment. She found temporary work as a program specialist. She hardly ever follows public affairs and she does not care very much how the presidential election turns out. Furthermore, she rarely discusses politics with family or friends. She watches television news three or four times a week and she does follow stories about the election. She reads *The State* daily and she follows some of the stories about the election. Likewise, she listens to election news reports on the radio, but she reads very few news magazines. In 1988, she did not vote, but her initial questionnaire reflected support for President Bush's re-election.

In her initial interview on July 23, 1994, Penny described political parties in terms of their membership: "Well, I think people are always going to be divided. Well, maybe not, because a lot of people like Perot. But, I don't know. I think you need to be a Democrat or Republican, one or the other. I don't really go with the independent idea." In terms of her own party affiliation, Penny said, "I basically consider myself a Republican because that's the way I was brought up. Basically, because that's all I ever heard from my dad." She said the most important issues facing the country are "the abortion issue and the economy, I guess, you know so many people unemployed and that kind of thing." She said unemployment was the most important "because, ya there are a lot of people affected by abortion, but they're still going to make their choices I guess. But unemployment you don't really have a choice. You're just unemployed." She said the first place she would go for news information is television, but she trusts news information from the radio.

Craig Koll, 26, a divorced father with a high school education who works as a receiving clerk. He does not follow government and public affairs closely, and he is not very interested in the campaign this year. Moreover, he rarely discusses political matters with family or friends. He watches national news stories about the campaign three or four times a week and he does follow other election news programs. He reads *The State* daily and he looks over some of the stories about the campaign. He listens to several speeches and conversations about the campaign on the radio, but he does not read any news magazines. In 1988 he did not vote in the presidential election, and he is undecided who to vote for in the 1992 election according to he initial questionnaire.

In his initial interview on July 22, 1994, Craig laughed and said the words political party had "no meaning at all" to him. He said he had no party affiliation and "to tell you the truth, until this Perot guy came into politics, I had no interest in it and tried to avoid it actually. He just made it interesting, because he was someone who just came, well not off the street, but with no political background." Craig said the most important problems facing the country were "jobs, I suppose, the recession going on, maybe the big thing is homelessness, abortion, so many things, God! The biggest thing with everybody seems to be money anyway. Everybody wants jobs and better jobs and lower taxes. Seems like the better jobs you get, the more taxes you have to pay out. I would guess that would have to be it, jobs." He said he trusted the newspapers the most, but he watches ABC News for national stories and channel 10 (WIS) for local information.

Elaine Miller, 41, a divorced mother with a high school education who was recently laid off from her job. She is currently working part time in a marketing position and she has gone back to school in order to finish her college degree. She follows public affairs infrequently and is only marginally interested in the campaign this year. She rarely talks about politics with her family or friends. She watches television news three or four times a week and she does follow other television programs about the campaign. She only reads *The State* about once a week, but she closely follows election coverage on the radio. She also reads about the election in several news magazines. In 1988, she did not vote, but she expressed a preference for Governor Clinton in her initial questionnaire.

In her initial interview on July 20, 1994, Elaine said political parties were "really arbitrary distinctions for me." She further stated, "I have mixed feelings about most issues, I mean, I'm not a straight party person, but I do usually find myself falling on the Democratic side. I know there are Republican philosophies that are beneficial, but I'm one of the poor people. I'm sorry." When asked to identify the most important problems facing America, she said, "I feel like you just asked me to describe God and the meaning of life. Well, the media puts it in your head. We're being told the biggest issue is unemployment and the economy. I just don't think its showing foresight or wisdom to isolate one issue. Although I will say this, I have been unemployed or under-employed for the majority of the last 24 months. And it is a nightmare, it really is. But that is a real pertinent issue and that's going to be the thing that sways the most voters." She said she seeks news information on major new events from CNN and National Public Radio, but she trusts information from "*The Utney,* a left leaning journal which is kind of an anthology of other sources."

Bill Nystrum, 45, married, a computer programmer with a Master's degree. He owns his own home in a deteriorating neighborhood. He follows public affairs some of the time, but he is not much interested in the 1992 election. He does not care personally about the outcome of the campaign, because he says "politics is hopeless." He watches television news three or four times a week and he follows stories and programs about the election. He reads *The State* daily, but adds that the paper "is not to be believed." He follows election stories in news magazines and on radio more frequently with a less skeptical eye. In 1988, he did not vote and he claims there has been "no one worth voting for in living memory." In his initial questionnaire, he expressed support for Ross Perot "for a change." In his initial interview on July 19, 1994, Mr. Nystrum stated that he was an independent. He said, "I can express my reasons, you know. But I think there are very many people out there who are not articulate, who have simply learned that the Democrats aren't it and the Republicans aren't it either." When asked to identify the most important problem facing America, he said: "Well. OK, here we go. The debt is not something that is just there. It is a symptom too. It takes one generation for any civilization to collapse just by failing to raise its young. One generation, it doesn't matter how many generations it's gone on, but we're working on it. With the underage population around here, in fact, we're preparing the house for market. It's not possible to relax properly here. We've got a great many crises coming up on us. If our economy collapses that's going to render all the rest of them almost intractable." He said he trusted National Public Radio and the news on "instructional television" the most.

Table 3.17 Low interest, difficult access group

Name (fictional)	Age	Race/Sex	Education	Occupation
Darlene Ross	28	WF	High School	Unemployed
Deidre Utley	33	WF	High School	Secretary
Sandra Sandelius	36	HF	College	Graduate Student
Bettie Tisdale	50	BF	Grade School	Unemployed

Darlene Ross, 28, single, a high school graduate who was recently laid off from her clerical position and forced to move back in with relatives in order to make ends meet. She rarely follows public affairs and she does not care personally how the 1992 election turns out. She discusses politics with family and friends only now and then. Likewise, she does not keep up regularly with any news sources. She does not watch television news and she only reads *The State* one or two times a week. Darlene does not read any news magazines, but she does hear some news broadcasts on her car radio while driving. In 1988, she did not vote, but she expressed support for President Bush in her questionnaire.

In her initial interview on July 21, 1994, Darlene described political parties by saying, "Republicans are rich and more out for themselves, I guess. Democrats are more down to earth and for the working people. Independent is people who are tired of both parties. That's it." She said she was not a member of either party and that she "votes for the best one." When asked to identify the most important problem facing the country, she responded, "the economy. I don't really see any other problems." She said NBC news was the source she trusted the most.

Deidre Utley, 33, married, an administrative assistant with a high school education. She follows government and public affairs only now and then and she is only somewhat interested in the 1992 presidential election. She talks about politics with family and friends infrequently, and she only manages to watch television news once a week. Deidre reads *The State,* about twice a week, but she does not listen to radio news and she does not read news magazines. She explains that working and raising a young son leave little time for news gathering. In 1988, she voted for George Bush and in her initial questionnaire she expressed support for his re-election.

In her initial interview on July 22, 1994, Deidre said political parties "are the way the government is run. The Republican party, to me, is headed up by one person and decisions are made by one person. I think of the Democratic party as being made up by a group of people and decided as such." She does not really consider herself a member of a party, but she said "I'd be a Republican if I had to choose." When asked to identify the most important problems facing America, she responded, "the budget, poverty, homeless." She said she trusted CNN the most, "because they send reporters to the action. They pretty much report things clearly. I just trust them."

Sandra Sandelius, 36, married, a medical student who lives with her husband in a large luxury apartment complex. She attempts to keep up with public affairs, but she is not much interested in the 1992 presidential election. She rarely discusses politics with family and friends. She watches television news and reads either *The State* or *The Washington Post* about once a week. Although she subscribes to news magazines, she does not have time to read them remarking that "they just pile up in the corner." She does not follow the campaign on radio. In 1988, she voted for George Bush, but in her initial questionnaire she remained uncommitted.

In her initial interview on July 20, 1994, Sandra said, "in general, Well, I believe a political party is an association of people who have the same ideals and want to drive for excellence in government and politics." She said, "I'm not affiliated with any party." When asked to identify the major problems facing America today, she said, "One is the isolation. In the sense that Americans are not liked overseas. I have suffered that experience myself. They see an American passport or American money and they don't like that. On the other side, Americans believe they have the answers and that is not always the case." She said she trusted "CNN and the BBC of London" the most.

Bettie Tisdale, 50, a single mother with a 9th grade education who is solely dependent on public assistance. She lives in a public housing complex with a high crime rate. She is somewhat interested in government and public affairs, but mostly on the local level. She is poorly informed about national and state politics, but she has a passing interest in the 1992 presidential election. She turns on the television news each day, but she is usually out of the room cooking, cleaning, or talking on the phone and too busy to pay attention to what is being broadcast. Bettie reads *The State* about once a week when she can get a copy and she occasionally reads about the election in a news magazine. In 1988, she could not remember for sure who she voted for, and she expressed support for President Bush in 1992.

In her initial interview on July 21, 1994, Bettie said she did not consider herself a member of a political party. She said, "I'm just a human being and a citizen of the United States. I'm not associated with either side. Democrat, I don't know nothing about that. What's the other one? Republican, I don't know who's right and who's wrong. I don't know nothing about that. See? I'm not concerned with that. I've got a kid to feed." When asked to identify the major problems facing the country, she said, "the main thing that I'm gonna feel about is these drugs and these young kids. That's why I like President Bush, because I feel, if he wasn't qualified, he wouldn't have the job in the first place. But the president doesn't have nothing to do with that. He's trying to stop the drugs, but I don't think he's going about it in the right way. You've got to get the head man that's bringing it into the kids. You know? If you don't get them, but I ain't interested in all this politics." She said she trusted channel 10 (WIS) the most, "but I like to watch that show America's Most Wanted. I might see somebody around here on it and I'd call it in."

Having now introduced the panelists and having explored the local political setting, the next section, Chapter 4, will report the findings of the news media content analysis. Chapter 5 presents the panelist interview findings. Once again, when specific incidents are mentioned in either Chapter 4 or Chapter 5, it may be helpful for the reader to refer back to Chapter 2 in order to remember the context in which the event took place.

Notes:

[1] ShoeMaker, Pamela J. and Stephen D. Reese, "Exposure to What? Integrating Media Content and Effects," *Journalism Quarterly* 64:4, Winter 1990:649-652.

[2] Sabato, Larry J. *Feeding Frenzy: How Attack Journalism Has Transformed American Politics*, 1st edition, The Free Press, 1992:6.

[3] Carullo, Julie *South Carolina Statistical Abstract*, South Carolina State Budget and Control Board-Division of Research and Statistical Services, 1993:321.

[4] Hoffman, Mark S. *World Almanac and Book of Facts 1993*, 1st edition, Pharos Books, 1993.

[5] Ibid:205

[6] Ibid:210

[7] See Black, Earl and Merle Black, *The Vital South: How Presidents are Elected*, 1st edition, Harvard University Press, 1992.

[8] Graham, Cole Blease,Jr. "Partisan Change in South Carolina," in *The South's New Politics: Realignment and Dealignment*, 1st edition, University of South Carolina Press, 1988:159.

[9] Ibid:160.

[10] Ibid:174.

[11] See sample questionnaire in appendix.

[12] See Kane, Eileen, *Doing Your Own Research: How to do basic research in the social sciences and humanities*, 2nd edition, Marion Boyars,1985:86-89; Dillman, Don A. *Mail and Telephone Surveys: The Total Design Method*, 1st edition, John Wiley & Sons, 1978:119-159; Sudman, Seymore and Norman M. Bradburn, *Asking Questions: A Practical Guide to Questionnaire Design*, 1st edition, Jossey-Bass Inc., 1982:261-280; and Warwick, Donald P. and Charles A. Lininger, *The Sample Survey: Theory and Practice*, 1st edition, McGraw-Hill, 1975:126-181.

[13] Warwick, Donald P. and Charles A. Lininger, *The Sample Survey Theory and Practice*, 1st edition, McGraw-Hill, 1975:129.

[14] Kane, Eileen, *Doing Your Own Research*, 2nd edition, Marion Boyars, 1985:87.

[15] Ibid:72

[16] Bernick, E. Lee and David J. Pratto, "Improving the Quality of Information in Mail Surveys: Use of Special Mailings," *Social Science Quarterly*, March 1994, 75,1:212.

[17]Ornstein, Norman, Andrew Kohut, and Larry McCarthy, *The People, the Press, & Politics,* Addison-Wesley Publishing, Inc., 1988:61.

[18]Kohut, Andrew, *The New Political Landscape,* Times Mirror Center for The People & The Press, October 1994:110.

[19]See Johnson, Janet Buttolph, and Richard A. Joslyn *Political Science Research Methods,* 1st edition, CQ Press, 1986:230.

[20]Strate, John M., Coit Cook Ford III, and Thomas B. Jankowski, "Women's Use of the Print Media to Follow Politics," *Social Science Quarterly,* March 1994, 75,1:166-186.

[21]Graber, Doris A. *Processing the News: How People Tame the Information Tide,* 1st edition, Longman, 1984:32.

[22]Black, Earl and Merle Black, *The Vital South,* 1st edition, Harvard University Press, 1992:7.

[23]Graham, Cole Blease, Jr. "Partisan Change in South Carolina" in *The South's New Politics,* 1st edition, University of South Carolina Press, 1988:159.

[24]Hoffman, Mark S. *World Almanac and Book of Facts 1993,* 1st edition, Pharos Books, 1992:191.

[25]Graber, Doris A. *Processing the News,* 1st edition, Longman, 1984:34.

[26]See Phillips, Kevin, *The Politics of Rich and Poor,: Wealth and the American Electorate in the Reagan Aftermath,* 1st edition, Random House, 1990.

[27]See Krippendorff, Klaus, *Content Analysis: An Introduction to Its Methodology,* 1st edition, Sage Publications, 1980.

[28]Graber, Doris A. *Processing The News,* 1st edition, Longman Press, 1984:21.

[29]See Gorden, Raymond L. *Interviewing: Strategy, Techniques and Tactics,* 1st edition, Dorsey Press,1969:37-54 ; Benjamin, Alfred *The Helping Interview,* 1st edition, Houghton Mifflin Company, 1974; and Graber, Doris A. *Processing the News,* 1st edition, Longman, 1984:16-19.

[30]Johnson, Janet Buttolph, and Richard A. Joslyn *Political Science Research Methods,* 1st edition, CQ Press, 1986:90.

Chapter 4

News Media Content Analysis

The content analysis of the news media sources consumed by the eighteen panelists in this study began on July 1, 1992 (approximately two weeks before the start of the panelist interviews). This allowed for a consistent interval of news accumulation during the interview routine since individual interviews of each panelist began after the Democratic National Convention and continued in two week interludes throughout the general election. This news media content analysis will be utilized in Chapter 5 in order to determine whether or not attack news items about the candidates reached all panel members regardless of political interest or media access and whether or not attack news stories affected the voting behavior of any of the 18 panelists.

The following panelist news sources were monitored: *The State*, a Knight-Ridder newspaper, published in Columbia, South Carolina; WIS-TV News, the local NBC affiliate which consistently draws the largest audience share in the Columbia market; and the national news broadcasts of ABC, CBS, and NBC as presented by the television news index and abstracts printed by the Vanderbilt Television News Archive. All news items from each news source were coded and placed into one of sixty four different categories. Tables 4.1–4.7 each contain a complete listing of the categories. Stories from each news source about Bush, Clinton, and Perot were broken down even further into attack items.

Chapter Organization

This chapter will begin with a report of the findings from each news source separately. First, data from the news content analysis of *The State* newspaper will be reviewed. Second, the news content information of WIS-TV will described. Third, data from the news content analysis of ABC, CBS, and NBC will be disclosed. After a summary of the findings from each news source, the chapter will then provide an analysis of candidate attack items over time as well as any similarities or differences between print and electronic media and national and local sources.

The State

A total of 12,955 news items were coded from *The State* newspaper from July 1 to November 3, 1992. As Table 4.1 shows, the Democratic Convention in July generated enough stories for Clinton to nearly equal the number of items about Bush, but the incumbent President clearly dominated the coverage from August until the end of the election. Articles about Perot dropped close to zero in August and September upon his hiatus from the campaign trail. Perot items picked up considerably in October upon his re-entry into the campaign.

Typically, candidates for the vice presidency receive less than 5% of the political coverage in the press. The 1992 Vice Presidential candidates received limited coverage in *The State*. The total number of articles for each candidate: Dan Quayle, Al Gore, and James Stockdale never exceeded 1% of the total items coded each month. This finding is consistent with a similar content analysis of another newspaper, the *Louisville Courier-Journal,* conducted during the 1992 presidential election by Staten and Sloss. In their study, of all articles surveyed, the percentage of paragraphs devoted to Dan Quayle was 2.2%, the percentage of paragraphs mentioning Al Gore was 1.0%, and the percentage of paragraphs concerning James Stockdale was 0.3%.[1]

The 18 panelists in this study consistently cited the economic condition of the country as well as George Bush's job performance concerning domestic issues as matters of importance during the campaign. This is important for two reasons. First, if the press highlights information concerning poor economic conditions and then fails to balance these articles with stories about economic recovery, voters may unfairly punish an incumbent president at the polls. Second, the economic conditions of the country may cause voters to focus more on issues and less on attack journalism.

Overall, as seen in Table 4.1, the number of stories in *The State* about the condition of the American economy decreased over time. For example, there were 74 news items reflecting the status of the U.S. economy in August making up 2.3% of the total number of items coded for the month. By October, 1992, the number of items concerning the

TABLE 4.1 THE STATE – 1992

	JULY	%	AUGUST	%	SEPTEMBER	%	OCTOBER	%	NOVEMBER	%	TOTALS	%
GOVT/POLITICS	14	0.5%	17	0.5%	15	0.5%	33	1.0%	9	2.8%	88	0.7%
ELECTIONS	36	1.2%	43	1.4%	58	1.8%	95	2.9%	22	6.9%	254	2.0%
BUSH	49	1.6%	74	2.3%	85	2.7%	108	3.3%	16	5.0%	332	2.6%
QUAYLE	14	0.5%	21	0.7%	19	0.6%	11	0.3%	0	0.0%	65	0.5%
CLINTON	47	1.5%	31	1.0%	65	2.0%	65	2.0%	7	2.2%	215	1.7%
GORE	9	0.3%	3	0.1%	8	0.3%	10	0.3%	1	0.3%	31	0.2%
PEROT	39	1.3%	10	0.3%	19	0.6%	43	1.3%	6	1.9%	117	0.9%
STOCKDALE	2	0.1%	0	0.0%	0	0.0%	4	0.1%	0	0.0%	6	0.0%
FAMILIES	9	0.3%	2	0.1%	5	0.2%	4	0.1%	0	0.0%	20	0.2%
DEMOCRATS	59	1.9%	7	0.2%	8	0.3%	12	0.4%	1	0.3%	87	0.7%
REPUBLICANS	5	0.2%	65	2.1%	16	0.5%	115	3.6%	2	0.6%	203	1.6%
POLLS	7	0.2%	6	0.2%	12	0.4%	14	0.4%	2	0.6%	41	0.3%
HOLLINGS	8	0.3%	5	0.2%	11	0.3%	21	0.6%	1	0.3%	46	0.4%
HARTNETT	9	0.3%	7	0.2%	8	0.3%	19	0.6%	1	0.3%	44	0.3%
CONGRESS. RACES	20	0.7%	41	1.3%	11	0.3%	40	1.2%	1	0.3%	113	0.9%
STATE/LOCAL	17	0.6%	80	2.5%	29	0.9%	25	0.8%	5	1.8%	156	1.2%
MEDIA & POLITICS	11	0.4%	14	0.4%	17	0.5%	29	0.9%	4	1.3%	75	0.6%
MILITARY	21	0.7%	36	1.1%	33	1.0%	27	0.8%	1	0.3%	118	0.9%
ARMY	7	0.2%	6	0.2%	3	0.1%	4	0.1%	0	0.0%	20	0.2%
NAVY	12	0.4%	16	0.5%	6	0.2%	6	0.2%	0	0.0%	40	0.3%
AIR FORCE	6	0.2%	8	0.3%	8	0.3%	6	0.2%	0	0.0%	28	0.2%
MARINES	1	0.0%	5	0.2%	2	0.1%	1	0.0%	0	0.0%	9	0.1%
VETERANS	9	0.3%	8	0.3%	10	0.3%	3	0.1%	0	0.0%	30	0.2%
FEDERAL GOVT.	32	1.0%	34	1.1%	33	1.0%	29	0.9%	1	0.3%	129	1.0%
STATE GOVT.	45	1.5%	55	1.7%	51	1.6%	21	0.6%	2	0.6%	174	1.3%
LOCAL GOVT.	42	1.4%	40	1.3%	35	1.1%	41	1.3%	2	0.6%	160	1.2%
INTERNATIONAL	237	7.7%	285	9.0%	226	7.1%	212	6.5%	21	6.6%	981	7.6%
ECONOMIC ISSUES	1	0.0%	2	0.1%	3	0.1%	13	0.4%	3	0.9%	22	0.2%
STATUS OF ECONOMY	52	1.7%	74	2.3%	46	1.4%	29	0.9%	3	0.9%	204	1.6%
BUSINESS	193	6.3%	164	5.2%	191	6.0%	216	6.7%	21	6.6%	785	6.1%
LABOR	26	0.8%	24	0.8%	33	1.0%	34	1.1%	2	0.6%	119	0.9%
CONSUMERS	9	0.3%	8	0.3%	12	0.4%	14	0.4%	0	0.0%	43	0.3%
ENVIRONMENT	58	1.9%	48	1.5%	47	1.5%	30	0.9%	5	1.6%	186	1.4%
ENERGY	20	0.7%	7	0.2%	23	0.7%	15	0.5%	1	0.3%	66	0.5%
TRANSPORTATION	14	0.5%	16	0.5%	18	0.6%	21	0.6%	2	0.6%	71	0.5%
HEALTH	118	3.9%	86	2.7%	124	3.9%	106	3.3%	13	4.1%	447	3.5%

SOCIAL ISSUES	0	0.0%	0	0.0%	0	0.0%	0	0.0%	0	0.0%	0	0.0%
ABORTION	22	0.7%	15	0.5%	8	0.3%	11	0.3%	1	0.3%	57	0.4%
EDUCATION	65	2.1%	89	2.8%	105	3.3%	102	3.2%	5	1.6%	366	2.8%
RELIGION	51	1.7%	52	1.6%	54	1.7%	50	1.5%	6	1.9%	213	1.6%
LAW ENFORCEMENT	51	1.7%	43	1.4%	58	1.8%	63	1.9%	4	1.3%	219	1.7%
CORRUPTION	34	1.1%	50	1.6%	47	1.5%	34	1.1%	1	0.3%	166	1.3%
INDIVIDUAL CRIME	169	5.5%	120	3.8%	109	3.4%	88	2.7%	11	3.5%	497	3.8%
SECURITY	0	0.0%	2	0.1%	4	0.1%	11	0.3%	4	1.3%	21	0.2%
DISASTERS	15	0.5%	58	1.8%	65	2.0%	22	0.7%	0	0.0%	160	1.2%
ACCIDENTS	45	1.5%	42	1.3%	27	0.8%	41	1.3%	5	1.6%	160	1.2%
DEPRIVED GROUPS	54	1.8%	54	1.7%	37	1.2%	36	1.1%	2	0.6%	183	1.4%
HUMAN INTEREST	103	3.4%	79	2.5%	89	2.8%	105	3.2%	8	2.5%	384	3.0%
CELEBRITIES	71	2.3%	84	2.7%	75	2.4%	55	1.7%	9	2.8%	294	2.3%
SCIENCE	26	0.8%	22	0.7%	30	0.9%	33	1.0%	3	0.9%	114	0.9%
T.V. SHOWS	20	0.7%	34	1.1%	32	1.0%	34	1.1%	1	0.3%	121	0.9%
MOVIES	30	1.0%	48	1.5%	39	1.2%	40	1.2%	3	0.9%	160	1.2%
SPORTS	133	4.3%	93	2.9%	104	3.3%	103	3.2%	10	3.2%	443	3.4%
BASEBALL	129	4.2%	131	4.2%	190	6.0%	123	3.8%	4	1.3%	577	4.5%
BASKETBALL	20	0.7%	22	0.7%	7	0.2%	42	1.3%	7	2.2%	98	0.8%
FOOTBALL	58	1.9%	162	5.1%	310	9.7%	287	8.9%	33	10.4%	850	6.6%
TENNIS	39	1.3%	17	0.5%	29	0.9%	1	0.0%	0	0.0%	86	0.7%
AUTO RACING	42	1.4%	24	0.8%	38	1.2%	29	0.9%	3	0.9%	136	1.0%
GOLF	50	1.6%	46	1.5%	11	0.3%	21	0.6%	1	0.3%	129	1.0%
OLYMPICS	128	4.2%	96	3.0%	0	0.0%	0	0.0%	0	0.0%	224	1.7%
ARTS	68	2.2%	78	2.5%	102	3.2%	109	3.4%	11	3.5%	368	2.8%
FOOD	49	1.6%	37	1.2%	47	1.5%	28	0.9%	1	0.3%	162	1.3%
COMICS (SECTION)	31	1.0%	31	1.0%	34	1.1%	31	1.0%	3	0.9%	130	1.0%
NOTICES	179	5.8%	156	4.9%	136	4.3%	158	4.9%	13	4.1%	642	5.0%
ADVICE COLUMNS	121	4.0%	124	3.9%	108	3.4%	104	3.2%	13	4.1%	470	3.6%
TOTALS	3,061	100.0%	3,155	100.0%	3,185	100.0%	3,237	100.0%	317	100.0%	12,955	100.0%

American economic situation had dropped to 29 making up only 0.9% of the total items coded that month. This finding seems to support Smith's contention in *The Vanishing Economy* that as economic conditions improve, economic news coverage progressively declines[2].

WIS-TV

A total of 2,384 items were coded from the 11:00 p.m. news broadcast of WIS-TV. This was the common local news broadcast watched by all the panelists in this study. Again, it is important to note that WIS-TV News is the dominant news broadcast in the Columbia market. Thus, it is not unusual that the panelists in this study followed the channel 10 news.

As Table 4.2 demonstrates, a month by month progression of WIS-TV news coverage of Bush, Clinton, and Perot shows that the number of Bush items dominated the months of August and September of 1992. Clinton received the most candidate coverage during the months of July and October of 1992. The increased coverage of Clinton during July of 1992 might be expected since the Democratic National Convention helped to showcase his candidacy that month. However, the increased coverage local news coverage of Clinton in October of 1992 may support the charges of a "bandwagon effect" among the media for Clinton once polls showed him ahead later in the general election. As seen with *The State* newspaper items, Perot stories on WIS-TV News dropped dramatically during the month of August, 1992 due to his withdrawal from the campaign. As Table 4.2 shows, Perot coverage on WIS gradually picked up from September to October, 1992 upon his re-entry into the race...

The proportion of coverage concerning the status of the economy on WIS-TV News was about equal to that of *The State*. Items involving the status of the economy on WIS made up less than 2% of the total items broadcast each month. The limited coverage might be explained by the local focus of the station and finite broadcast time. Moreover, local news broadcasts devote more time to sports and weather leaving confined space for national issues which news directors may feel are adequately covered by their national affiliates.

Network Television News

Since the panelists in this study followed a variety of different national news programs, this study includes a separate content analysis

TABLE 4.2 WIS–TV – 1992	JULY	%	AUGUST	%	SEPT.	%	OCT.	%	NOV.	%	TOTAL	%
Govt./Politics	0	0.0%	1	0.0%	2	0.2%	1	0.2%	0	0.0%	4	0.2%
Elections	3	0.5%	4	0.5%	3	0.7%	9	1.5%	2	5.1%	21	0.9%
Bush	9	1.5%	16	1.5%	21	2.7%	22	3.8%	2	5.1%	70	2.9%
Quayle	2	0.3%	3	0.3%	4	0.5%	1	0.2%	0	0.0%	10	0.4%
Clinton	15	2.6%	6	2.6%	15	1.0%	28	4.8%	4	10.3%	68	2.9%
Gore	1	0.2%	0	0.2%	2	0.0%	10	1.7%	0	0.0%	13	0.5%
Perot	12	2.1%	1	2.1%	8	0.2%	19	3.3%	4	10.3%	44	1.8%
Stockdale	0	0.0%	0	0.0%	0	0.0%	1	0.2%	0	0.0%	1	0.0%
Families	0	0.0%	0	0.0%	0	0.0%	0	0.0%	0	0.0%	0	0.0%
Dems	16	2.7%	2	2.7%	3	0.3%	5	0.9%	0	0.0%	26	1.1%
GOP	4	0.7%	12	0.7%	2	2.0%	0	0.0%	0	0.0%	18	0.8%
Polls	7	1.2%	2	1.2%	7	0.3%	14	2.4%	1	2.6%	31	1.3%
Hollings	1	0.2%	0	0.2%	5	0.0%	11	1.9%	0	0.0%	17	0.7%
Hartnett	0	0.0%	1	0.0%	7	0.2%	11	1.9%	0	0.0%	19	0.8%
Cong. Races	0	0.0%	3	0.0%	0	0.5%	2	0.3%	0	0.0%	5	0.2%
State & Local	4	0.7%	6	0.7%	8	1.0%	2	0.3%	0	0.0%	20	0.8%
Media & Politics	3	0.5%	4	0.5%	1	0.7%	13	2.2%	0	0.0%	21	0.9%
Military	9	1.5%	11	1.5%	10	1.9%	9	1.5%	1	2.6%	40	1.7%
Army	0	0.0%	0	0.0%	1	0.0%	0	0.0%	0	0.0%	1	0.0%
Navy	2	0.3%	0	0.3%	1	0.0%	0	0.0%	0	0.0%	3	0.1%
Air Force	1	0.2%	2	0.2%	1	0.3%	1	0.2%	0	0.0%	5	0.2%
Marines	0	0.0%	0	0.0%	1	0.0%	0	0.0%	0	0.0%	1	0.0%
Vets	0	0.0%	0	0.0%	1	0.0%	0	0.0%	0	0.0%	1	0.0%
Federal Govt.	2	0.3%	1	0.3%	5	0.2%	0	0.0%	0	0.0%	8	0.3%
State Govt.	16	2.7%	17	2.7%	18	2.9%	13	2.2%	0	0.0%	64	2.7%
Local Govt.	1	0.2%	2	0.2%	2	0.3%	2	0.3%	0	0.0%	7	0.3%
International	21	3.6%	23	3.6%	20	3.9%	14	2.4%	1	2.6%	79	3.3%
Economic Issues	3	0.5%	2	0.5%	2	0.3%	1	0.2%	0	0.0%	8	0.3%
Status of Economy	11	1.9%	10	1.9%	10	1.7%	10	1.7%	0	0.0%	41	1.7%
Business	13	2.2%	10	2.2%	14	1.7%	16	2.7%	1	2.6%	54	2.3%
Labor	1	0.2%	0	0.2%	3	0.0%	2	0.3%	0	0.0%	6	0.3%

Category	N	%	N	%	N	%	N	%	N	%	N	%
Consumers	3	0.5%	3	0.5%	6	1.0%	5	0.9%	1	2.6%	18	0.8%
Environment	7	1.2%	8	1.4%	6	1.0%	9	1.5%	0	0.0%	30	1.3%
Energy	0	0.0%	0	0.0%	0	0.0%	0	0.0%	0	0.0%	0	0.0%
Transportation	2	0.3%	3	0.5%	5	0.9%	3	0.5%	1	2.6%	14	0.6%
Health	33	5.6%	31	5.2%	33	5.6%	37	6.3%	2	5.1%	136	5.7%
Social Issues	0	0.0%	0	0.0%	1	0.2%	1	0.2%	0	0.0%	2	0.1%
Abortion	8	1.4%	2	0.3%	1	0.2%	3	0.5%	0	0.0%	14	0.6%
Education	7	1.2%	9	1.5%	8	1.4%	8	1.4%	2	5.1%	32	1.3%
Religion	7	1.2%	8	1.4%	6	1.0%	7	1.2%	1	2.6%	30	1.3%
Law Enforcement	18	3.1%	20	3.4%	24	4.1%	22	3.8%	0	0.0%	85	3.6%
Corruption	0	0.0%	9	1.5%	5	0.9%	2	0.3%	2	5.1%	16	0.7%
Individual Crime	34	5.8%	31	5.2%	36	6.2%	28	4.8%	0	0.0%	131	5.5%
Security	0	0.0%	1	0.2%	0	0.0%	0	0.0%	0	0.0%	1	0.0%
Disasters	1	0.2%	23	3.9%	24	4.1%	8	1.4%	1	2.6%	56	2.3%
Accidents	12	2.1%	11	1.9%	4	0.7%	7	1.2%	0	0.0%	35	1.5%
Deprived Groups	1	0.2%	4	0.7%	6	1.0%	1	0.2%	1	2.6%	12	0.5%
Human Interest	10	1.7%	11	1.9%	10	1.7%	13	2.2%	0	0.0%	45	1.9%
Celebrities	2	0.3%	4	0.7%	3	0.5%	4	0.7%	0	0.0%	13	0.5%
Science	2	0.3%	1	0.2%	4	0.7%	2	0.3%	0	0.0%	9	0.4%
TV Shows	15	2.6%	19	3.2%	15	2.6%	18	3.1%	1	2.6%	68	2.9%
Movies	6	1.0%	5	0.8%	5	0.9%	5	0.9%	0	0.0%	21	0.9%
Sports	40	6.8%	26	4.4%	5	0.9%	5	0.9%	0	0.0%	76	3.2%
Baseball	54	9.2%	51	8.6%	42	7.2%	23	3.9%	1	2.6%	171	7.2%
Basketball	3	0.5%	1	0.2%	8	1.4%	7	1.2%	1	2.6%	20	0.8%
Football	8	1.4%	32	5.4%	37	6.3%	50	8.6%	4	10.3%	131	5.5%
Tennis	11	1.9%	8	1.4%	14	2.4%	0	0.0%	0	0.0%	33	1.4%
Auto Racing	15	2.6%	6	1.0%	5	0.9%	6	1.0%	0	0.0%	32	1.3%
Golf	7	1.2%	8	1.4%	4	0.7%	1	0.2%	0	0.0%	20	0.8%
Olympics	32	5.5%	21	3.6%	0	0.0%	0	0.0%	0	0.0%	53	2.2%
Arts	0	0.0%	2	0.3%	5	0.9%	3	0.5%	0	0.0%	10	0.4%
Food	1	0.2%	2	0.3%	3	0.5%	1	0.2%	0	0.0%	7	0.3%
Notices	0	0.0%	0	0.0%	0	0.0%	0	0.0%	0	0.0%	0	0.0%
Editorials	0	0.0%	0	0.0%	0	0.0%	0	0.0%	0	0.0%	0	0.0%
Weather	89	15.2%	92	15.6%	83	14.2%	88	15.1%	5	12.8%	357	15.0%
TOTALS	585	100.0%	591	100.0%	585	100.0%	584	100.0%	39	100.0%	2,384	100.0%

of ABC News, CBS News, and NBC News. The amount of coverage involving the presidential candidates varied among each of the three networks, but never by more than one or two percentage points. Stories devoted to Clinton and Bush neared parity during the months of July and October of 1992. Bush dominated coverage during the months of August and September.of 1992. As seen with the other news sources in this study, coverage of Perot dropped off during the months of August and September of 1992, but increased during the months of October and November of 1992. Like both *The State* and WIS-TV, the amount of coverage devoted to the Vice Presidential contenders was 2% or less each month throughout the campaign.

However, in comparison to items in *The State* or on WIS-TV News, stories about the presidential candidates on the network news broadcasts made up a higher percentage of the total items. Each candidate rarely received over 2% of the total items each month in the newspaper or on the local broadcast news. The shear volume and variety of items in a daily newspaper helps to explain the relatively low percentage of articles about the presidential candidates. Furthermore, as mentioned earlier, local news broadcasts devote long segments to sports and weather and have limited time for national news.

However, as seen in Tables 4.3–4.7, individual candidate items on the network news broadcasts.ranged from 5.9% to 13.6% of the total items coded each month. Since the network news broadcasts provided a greater share of presidential campaign news information, panelists with difficult media access, who occasionally watched national news broadcasts, may have received enough exposure to the presidential contest to keep adequately informed. It is also important to investigate whether or not there are differences in the way the networks cover the campaign.

For example, in a content analysis of network television news coverage during the 1992 presidential election, Noyes, Lichter, and Amundson, utilizing a slightly different methodology, discovered that the tone of the news items was different for each candidate. During the convention phases of the campaign, Noyes, Lichter, and Amundson claim that Bush received positive news evaluations 30% of the time while Clinton received positive stories 50% of the time. Their study also found that these approximate percentages held consistent during the general election phase of the campaign.[3]

It is also important to note that the networks devoted a higher percentage of coverage to the status of the economy in comparison to

TABLE 4.3 JULY 1992	ABC	%	CBS	%	NBC	%	TOTAL	%
Govt./Politics	0	0.0%	0	0.0%	0	0.0%	0	0.0%
Elections	4	0.5%	9	1.2%	4	0.5%	17	0.7%
Bush	66	8.4%	75	9.7%	70	8.8%	211	9.0%
Quayle	8	1.0%	14	1.8%	16	2.0%	38	1.6%
Clinton	77	9.8%	67	8.7%	59	7.4%	203	8.6%
Gore	13	1.7%	6	0.8%	11	1.4%	30	1.3%
Perot	42	5.4%	56	7.3%	46	5.8%	144	6.1%
Stockdale	0	0.0%	0	0.0%	0	0.0%	0	0.0%
Families	6	0.8%	3	0.4%	3	0.4%	12	0.5%
Dems	51	6.5%	48	6.2%	31	3.9%	130	5.5%
GOP	9	1.1%	17	2.2%	10	1.3%	36	1.5%
Polls	5	0.6%	5	0.6%	6	0.8%	16	0.7%
Cong. Races	1	0.1%	5	0.6%	3	0.4%	9	0.4%
State & Local	0	0.0%	0	0.0%	1	0.1%	1	0.0%
Media & Politics	6	0.8%	8	1.0%	3	0.4%	17	0.7%
Military	42	5.4%	28	3.6%	29	3.7%	99	4.2%
Army	3	0.4%	3	0.4%	3	0.4%	9	0.4%
Navy	8	1.0%	8	1.0%	7	0.9%	23	1.0%
Air Force	3	0.4%	4	0.5%	0	0.0%	7	0.3%
Marines	0	0.0%	2	0.3%	0	0.0%	2	0.1%
Vets	2	0.3%	2	0.3%	0	0.0%	4	0.2%
International	83	10.6%	69	8.9%	85	10.7%	237	10.1%
Economic Issues	14	1.8%	7	0.9%	23	2.9%	44	1.9%
Status of Economy	29	3.7%	15	1.9%	31	3.9%	75	3.2%
Business	11	1.4%	12	1.6%	19	2.4%	42	1.8%
Labor	5	0.6%	5	0.6%	9	1.1%	19	0.8%
Consumers	6	0.8%	3	0.4%	4	0.5%	13	0.6%
Environment	13	1.7%	10	1.3%	16	2.0%	39	1.7%
Energy	1	0.1%	1	0.1%	0	0.0%	2	0.1%
Transportation	8	1.0%	11	1.4%	7	0.9%	26	1.1%
Health	52	6.6%	53	6.9%	44	5.5%	149	6.3%
Social Issues	2	0.3%	18	2.3%	7	0.9%	27	1.1%
Abortion	5	0.6%	8	1.0%	19	2.4%	32	1.4%
Education	12	1.5%	15	1.9%	3	0.4%	30	1.3%
Religion	5	0.6%	31	4.0%	13	1.6%	49	2.1%
Law Enforcement	12	1.5%	10	1.3%	22	2.8%	44	1.9%
Corruption	8	1.0%	12	1.6%	13	1.6%	33	1.4%
Individual Crime	12	1.5%	0	0.0%	25	3.1%	37	1.6%
Security	0	0.0%	5	0.6%	0	0.0%	5	0.2%
Disasters	4	0.5%	8	1.0%	3	0.4%	15	0.6%
Accidents	5	0.6%	18	2.3%	5	0.6%	28	1.2%
Deprived Groups	25	3.2%	14	1.8%	19	2.4%	58	2.5%
Human Interest	17	2.2%	3	0.4%	10	1.3%	30	1.3%
Celebrities	3	0.4%	7	0.9%	7	0.9%	17	0.7%
Science	9	1.1%	0	0.0%	5	0.6%	14	0.6%
TV Shows	0	0.0%	0	0.0%	0	0.0%	0	0.0%
Sports	9	1.1%	7	0.9%	4	0.5%	20	0.9%
Baseball	11	1.4%	8	1.0%	10	1.3%	29	1.2%
Basketball	0	0.0%	0	0.0%	0	0.0%	0	0.0%
Football	0	0.0%	0	0.0%	0	0.0%	0	0.0%
Tennis	3	0.4%	2	0.3%	2	0.3%	7	0.3%
Auto Racing	2	0.3%	0	0.0%	3	0.4%	5	0.2%
Golf	6	0.8%	0	0.0%	0	0.0%	6	0.3%
Olympics	27	3.4%	15	1.9%	45	5.7%	87	3.7%
Arts	9	1.1%	11	1.4%	5	0.6%	25	1.1%
Food	8	1.0%	3	0.4%	5	0.6%	16	0.7%
Notices	0	0.0%	0	0.0%	0	0.0%	0	0.0%
Editorials	0	0.0%	0	0.0%	1	0.1%	1	0.0%
Weather	0	0.0%	2	0.3%	1	0.1%	3	0.1%
TOTALS	784	100.0%	772	100.0%	794	100.0%	2,350	100.0%

TABLE 4.4 AUGUST 1992	ABC	%	CBS	%	NBC	%	TOTAL	%
Govt./Politics	4	0.4%	4	0.4%	4	0.4%	12	0.4%
Elections	6	0.5%	16	1.6%	7	0.7%	29	1.0%
Bush	143	13.1%	111	11.3%	137	14.5%	391	13.0%
Quayle	23	2.1%	10	1.0%	6	0.6%	39	1.3%
Clinton	64	5.9%	69	7.0%	62	6.6%	195	6.5%
Gore	8	0.7%	5	0.5%	8	0.8%	21	0.7%
Perot	3	0.3%	21	2.1%	7	0.7%	31	1.0%
Stockdale	0	0.0%	0	0.0%	0	0.0%	0	0.0%
Families	7	0.6%	8	0.8%	12	1.3%	27	0.9%
Dems	13	1.2%	8	0.8%	4	0.4%	25	0.8%
GOP	77	7.0%	68	6.9%	46	4.9%	191	6.3%
Polls	8	0.7%	14	1.4%	3	0.3%	25	0.8%
Cong. Races	1	0.1%	5	0.5%	7	0.7%	13	0.4%
State & Local	0	0.0%	0	0.0%	0	0.0%	0	0.0%
Media & Politics	9	0.8%	5	0.5%	1	0.1%	15	0.5%
Military	81	7.4%	69	7.0%	70	7.4%	220	7.3%
Army	0	0.0%	3	0.3%	5	0.5%	8	0.3%
Navy	7	0.6%	12	1.2%	1	0.1%	20	0.7%
Air Force	6	0.5%	3	0.3%	7	0.7%	16	0.5%
Marines	8	0.7%	4	0.4%	5	0.5%	17	0.6%
Vets	2	0.2%	3	0.3%	4	0.4%	9	0.3%
Federal Govt.	7	0.6%	1	0.1%	3	0.3%	11	0.4%
State Govt.	19	1.7%	5	0.5%	13	1.4%	37	1.2%
Local Govt.	8	0.7%	12	1.2%	9	1.0%	29	1.0%
International	117	10.7%	92	9.4%	81	8.6%	290	9.6%
Economic Issues	2	0.2%	2	0.2%	4	0.4%	8	0.3%
Status of Economy	57	5.2%	30	3.1%	28	3.0%	115	3.8%
Business	19	1.7%	26	2.7%	22	2.3%	67	2.2%
Labor	8	0.7%	5	0.5%	13	1.4%	26	0.9%
Consumers	2	0.2%	8	0.8%	14	1.5%	24	0.8%
Environment	24	2.2%	10	1.0%	9	1.0%	43	1.4%
Energy	0	0.0%	7	0.7%	3	0.3%	10	0.3%
Transportation	5	0.5%	17	1.7%	10	1.1%	32	1.1%
Health	38	3.5%	38	3.9%	35	3.7%	111	3.7%
Social Issues	5	0.5%	4	0.4%	4	0.4%	13	0.4%
Abortion	8	0.7%	2	0.2%	0	0.0%	10	0.3%
Education	3	0.3%	7	0.7%	16	1.7%	26	0.9%
Religion	3	0.3%	4	0.4%	0	0.0%	7	0.2%
Law Enforcement	18	1.6%	23	2.3%	36	3.8%	77	2.6%
Corruption	4	0.4%	0	0.0%	5	0.5%	9	0.3%
Individual Crime	18	1.6%	11	1.1%	25	2.6%	54	1.8%
Security	0	0.0%	0	0.0%	0	0.0%	0	0.0%
Disasters	62	5.7%	65	6.6%	50	5.3%	177	5.9%
Accidents	11	1.0%	11	1.1%	10	1.1%	32	1.1%
Deprived Groups	49	4.5%	51	5.2%	26	2.8%	126	4.2%
Human Interest	14	1.3%	10	1.0%	7	0.7%	31	1.0%
Celebrities	8	0.7%	12	1.2%	22	2.3%	42	1.4%
Science	9	0.8%	10	1.0%	14	1.5%	33	1.1%
TV Shows	0	0.0%	0	0.0%	0	0.0%	0	0.0%
Sports	4	0.4%	5	0.5%	5	0.5%	14	0.5%
Baseball	18	1.6%	1	0.1%	9	1.0%	28	0.9%
Basketball	2	0.2%	4	0.4%	6	0.6%	12	0.4%
Football	2	0.2%	4	0.4%	3	0.3%	9	0.3%
Tennis	7	0.6%	0	0.0%	0	0.0%	7	0.2%
Auto Racing	3	0.3%	0	0.0%	3	0.3%	6	0.2%
Golf	5	0.5%	0	0.0%	0	0.0%	5	0.2%
Olympics	36	3.3%	18	1.8%	38	4.0%	92	3.0%
Arts	7	0.6%	10	1.0%	1	0.1%	18	0.6%
Food	3	0.3%	4	0.4%	2	0.2%	9	0.3%
Notices	0	0.0%	0	0.0%	0	0.0%	0	0.0%
Editorials	0	0.0%	0	0.0%	0	0.0%	0	0.0%
Weather	19	1.7%	33	3.4%	22	2.3%	74	2.5%
TOTALS	1,094	100.0%	980	100.0%	944	100.0%	3,018	100.0%

TABLE 4.5 SEPTEMBER 1992	ABC	%	CBS	%	NBC	%	TOTAL	%
Govt./Politics	3	0.3%	5	0.5%	4	0.4%	12	0.4%
Elections	36	3.7%	20	2.0%	32	3.2%	88	3.0%
Bush	129	13.4%	119	11.9%	115	11.5%	363	12.3%
Quayle	17	1.8%	13	1.3%	12	1.2%	42	1.4%
Clinton	95	9.9%	99	9.9%	82	8.2%	276	9.3%
Gore	7	0.7%	4	0.4%	3	0.3%	14	0.5%
Perot	26	2.7%	21	2.1%	32	3.2%	79	2.7%
Stockdale	0	0.0%	0	0.0%	0	0.0%	0	0.0%
Families	4	0.4%	11	1.1%	5	0.5%	20	0.7%
Dems	7	0.7%	7	0.7%	3	0.3%	17	0.6%
GOP	6	0.6%	10	1.0%	6	0.6%	22	0.7%
Polls	7	0.7%	10	1.0%	8	0.8%	25	0.8%
Cong. Races	4	0.4%	23	2.3%	10	1.0%	37	1.3%
State & Local	2	0.2%	2	0.2%	7	0.7%	11	0.4%
Media & Politics	6	0.6%	4	0.4%	0	0.0%	10	0.3%
Military	29	3.0%	37	3.7%	38	3.8%	104	3.5%
Army	7	0.7%	9	0.9%	3	0.3%	19	0.6%
Navy	15	1.6%	6	0.6%	13	1.3%	34	1.2%
Air Force	4	0.4%	5	0.5%	1	0.1%	10	0.3%
Marines	0	0.0%	1	0.1%	1	0.1%	2	0.1%
Vets	3	0.3%	5	0.5%	0	0.0%	8	0.3%
Federal Govt.	6	0.6%	9	0.9%	3	0.3%	18	0.6%
State Govt.	16	1.7%	6	0.6%	9	0.9%	31	1.0%
Local Govt.	10	1.0%	23	2.3%	20	2.0%	53	1.8%
International	94	9.8%	105	10.5%	76	7.6%	275	9.3%
Economic Issues	11	1.1%	13	1.3%	21	2.1%	45	1.5%
Status of Economy	55	5.7%	28	2.8%	48	4.8%	131	4.4%
Business	10	1.0%	15	1.5%	23	2.3%	48	1.6%
Labor	8	0.8%	23	2.3%	24	2.4%	55	1.9%
Consumers	7	0.7%	16	1.6%	16	1.6%	39	1.3%
Environment	3	0.3%	6	0.6%	29	2.9%	38	1.3%
Energy	0	0.0%	1	0.1%	2	0.2%	3	0.1%
Transportation	3	0.3%	7	0.7%	0	0.0%	10	0.3%
Health	35	3.6%	64	6.4%	38	3.8%	137	4.6%
Social Issues	10	1.0%	18	1.8%	16	1.6%	44	1.5%
Abortion	5	0.5%	9	0.9%	5	0.5%	19	0.6%
Education	9	0.9%	7	0.7%	46	4.6%	62	2.1%
Religion	19	2.0%	13	1.3%	7	0.7%	39	1.3%
Law Enforcement	20	2.1%	17	1.7%	25	2.5%	62	2.1%
Corruption	3	0.3%	28	2.8%	15	1.5%	46	1.6%
Individual Crime	25	2.6%	20	2.0%	15	1.5%	60	2.0%
Security	0	0.0%	0	0.0%	0	0.0%	0	0.0%
Disasters	88	9.2%	78	7.8%	77	7.7%	243	8.2%
Accidents	4	0.4%	3	0.3%	14	1.4%	21	0.7%
Deprived Groups	13	1.4%	14	1.4%	13	1.3%	40	1.4%
Human Interest	2	0.2%	5	0.5%	11	1.1%	18	0.6%
Celebrities	5	0.5%	2	0.2%	7	0.7%	14	0.5%
Science	13	1.4%	5	0.5%	14	1.4%	32	1.1%
TV Shows	0	0.0%	4	0.4%	3	0.3%	7	0.2%
Sports	12	1.2%	1	0.1%	11	1.1%	24	0.8%
Baseball	17	1.8%	19	1.9%	17	1.7%	53	1.8%
Basketball	5	0.5%	5	0.5%	5	0.5%	15	0.5%
Football	20	2.1%	0	0.0%	1	0.1%	21	0.7%
Tennis	3	0.3%	5	0.5%	0	0.0%	8	0.3%
Auto Racing	0	0.0%	0	0.0%	0	0.0%	0	0.0%
Golf	7	0.7%	0	0.0%	0	0.0%	7	0.2%
Olympics	0	0.0%	0	0.0%	0	0.0%	0	0.0%
Arts	5	0.5%	3	0.3%	4	0.4%	12	0.4%
Food	9	0.9%	6	0.6%	1	0.1%	16	0.5%
Notices	0	0.0%	0	0.0%	0	0.0%	0	0.0%
Editorials	0	0.0%	0	0.0%	0	0.0%	0	0.0%
Weather	2	0.2%	7	0.7%	7	0.7%	16	0.5%
TOTALS	961	100.0%	996	100.0%	998	100.0%	2,955	100.0%

TABLE 4.6 OCTOBER 1992	ABC	%	CBS	%	NBC	%	TOTAL	%
Govt./Politics	11	1.1%	11	1.2%	11	1.0%	33	1.1%
Elections	24	2.4%	38	4.2%	42	3.9%	104	3.5%
Bush	124	12.4%	123	13.7%	151	14.1%	398	13.4%
Quayle	8	0.8%	10	1.1%	18	1.7%	36	1.2%
Clinton	127	12.7%	96	10.7%	121	11.3%	344	11.6%
Gore	12	1.2%	10	1.1%	20	1.9%	42	1.4%
Perot	57	5.7%	82	9.1%	80	7.5%	219	7.4%
Stockdale	5	0.5%	10	1.1%	5	0.5%	20	0.7%
Families	2	0.2%	1	0.1%	4	0.4%	7	0.2%
Dems	11	1.1%	13	1.4%	13	1.2%	37	1.2%
GOP	15	1.5%	25	2.8%	19	1.8%	59	2.0%
Polls	23	2.3%	17	1.9%	18	1.7%	58	2.0%
Cong. Races	21	2.1%	8	0.9%	18	1.7%	47	1.6%
State & Local	2	0.2%	1	0.1%	15	1.4%	18	0.6%
Media & Politics	13	1.3%	27	3.0%	20	1.9%	60	2.0%
Military	38	3.8%	23	2.6%	39	3.7%	100	3.4%
Army	0	0.0%	0	0.0%	0	0.0%	0	0.0%
Navy	2	0.2%	2	0.2%	4	0.4%	8	0.3%
Air Force	1	0.1%	1	0.1%	1	0.1%	3	0.1%
Marines	0	0.0%	0	0.0%	0	0.0%	0	0.0%
Vets	0	0.0%	0	0.0%	0	0.0%	0	0.0%
Federal Govt.	10	1.0%	2	0.2%	4	0.4%	16	0.5%
State Govt.	4	0.4%	4	0.4%	9	0.8%	17	0.6%
Local Govt.	16	1.6%	11	1.2%	19	1.8%	46	1.5%
International	107	10.7%	52	5.8%	68	6.4%	227	7.6%
Economic Issues	5	0.5%	13	1.4%	15	1.4%	33	1.1%
Status of Economy	42	4.2%	17	1.9%	35	3.3%	94	3.2%
Business	21	2.1%	11	1.2%	20	1.9%	52	1.8%
Labor	12	1.2%	17	1.9%	31	2.9%	60	2.0%
Consumers	1	0.1%	9	1.0%	2	0.2%	12	0.4%
Environment	15	1.5%	5	0.6%	15	1.4%	35	1.2%
Energy	7	0.7%	5	0.6%	0	0.0%	12	0.4%
Transportation	5	0.5%	1	0.1%	12	1.1%	18	0.6%
Health	44	4.4%	59	6.6%	41	3.8%	144	4.8%
Social Issues	2	0.2%	12	1.3%	10	0.9%	24	0.8%
Abortion	2	0.2%	11	1.2%	9	0.8%	22	0.7%
Education	13	1.3%	9	1.0%	11	1.0%	33	1.1%
Religion	10	1.0%	6	0.7%	8	0.7%	24	0.8%
Law Enforcement	22	2.2%	13	1.4%	20	1.9%	55	1.9%
Corruption	24	2.4%	25	2.8%	18	1.7%	67	2.3%
Individual Crime	14	1.4%	10	1.1%	32	3.0%	56	1.9%
Security	0	0.0%	0	0.0%	0	0.0%	0	0.0%
Disasters	11	1.1%	12	1.3%	19	1.8%	42	1.4%
Accidents	16	1.6%	14	1.6%	15	1.4%	45	1.5%
Deprived Groups	22	2.2%	23	2.6%	5	0.5%	50	1.7%
Human Interest	14	1.4%	9	1.0%	12	1.1%	35	1.2%
Celebrities	10	1.0%	4	0.4%	6	0.6%	20	0.7%
Science	15	1.5%	13	1.4%	9	0.8%	37	1.2%
TV Shows	2	0.2%	2	0.2%	0	0.0%	4	0.1%
Sports	5	0.5%	0	0.0%	2	0.2%	7	0.2%
Baseball	13	1.3%	25	2.8%	7	0.7%	45	1.5%
Basketball	1	0.1%	0	0.0%	0	0.0%	1	0.0%
Football	11	1.1%	0	0.0%	4	0.4%	15	0.5%
Tennis	0	0.0%	0	0.0%	0	0.0%	0	0.0%
Auto Racing	0	0.0%	0	0.0%	0	0.0%	0	0.0%
Golf	0	0.0%	0	0.0%	0	0.0%	0	0.0%
Olympics	0	0.0%	0	0.0%	0	0.0%	0	0.0%
Arts	4	0.4%	4	0.4%	1	0.1%	9	0.3%
Food	7	0.7%	1	0.1%	5	0.5%	13	0.4%
Notices	0	0.0%	0	0.0%	0	0.0%	0	0.0%
Editorials	0	0.0%	2	0.2%	0	0.0%	2	0.1%
Weather	0	0.0%	0	0.0%	5	0.5%	5	0.2%
TOTALS	1003	100.0%	899	100.0%	1068	100.0%	2,970	100.0%

TABLE 4.5 SEPTEMBER 1992	ABC	%	CBS	%	NBC	%	TOTAL	%
Govt./Politics	3	0.3%	5	0.5%	4	0.4%	12	0.4%
Elections	36	3.7%	20	2.0%	32	3.2%	88	3.0%
Bush	129	13.4%	119	11.9%	115	11.5%	363	12.3%
Quayle	17	1.8%	13	1.3%	12	1.2%	42	1.4%
Clinton	95	9.9%	99	9.9%	82	8.2%	276	9.3%
Gore	7	0.7%	4	0.4%	3	0.3%	14	0.5%
Perot	26	2.7%	21	2.1%	32	3.2%	79	2.7%
Stockdale	0	0.0%	0	0.0%	0	0.0%	0	0.0%
Families	4	0.4%	11	1.1%	5	0.5%	20	0.7%
Dems	7	0.7%	7	0.7%	3	0.3%	17	0.6%
GOP	6	0.6%	10	1.0%	6	0.6%	22	0.7%
Polls	7	0.7%	10	1.0%	8	0.8%	25	0.8%
Cong. Races	4	0.4%	23	2.3%	10	1.0%	37	1.3%
State & Local	2	0.2%	2	0.2%	7	0.7%	11	0.4%
Media & Politics	6	0.6%	4	0.4%	0	0.0%	10	0.3%
Military	29	3.0%	37	3.7%	38	3.8%	104	3.5%
Army	7	0.7%	9	0.9%	3	0.3%	19	0.6%
Navy	15	1.6%	6	0.6%	13	1.3%	34	1.2%
Air Force	4	0.4%	5	0.5%	1	0.1%	10	0.3%
Marines	0	0.0%	1	0.1%	1	0.1%	2	0.1%
Vets	3	0.3%	5	0.5%	0	0.0%	8	0.3%
Federal Govt.	6	0.6%	9	0.9%	3	0.3%	18	0.6%
State Govt.	16	1.7%	6	0.6%	9	0.9%	31	1.0%
Local Govt.	10	1.0%	23	2.3%	20	2.0%	53	1.8%
International	94	9.8%	105	10.5%	76	7.6%	275	9.3%
Economic Issues	11	1.1%	13	1.3%	21	2.1%	45	1.5%
Status of Economy	55	5.7%	28	2.8%	48	4.8%	131	4.4%
Business	10	1.0%	15	1.5%	23	2.3%	48	1.6%
Labor	8	0.8%	23	2.3%	24	2.4%	55	1.9%
Consumers	7	0.7%	16	1.6%	16	1.6%	39	1.3%
Environment	3	0.3%	6	0.6%	29	2.9%	38	1.3%
Energy	0	0.0%	1	0.1%	2	0.2%	3	0.1%
Transportation	3	0.3%	7	0.7%	0	0.0%	10	0.3%
Health	35	3.6%	64	6.4%	38	3.8%	137	4.6%
Social Issues	10	1.0%	18	1.8%	16	1.6%	44	1.5%
Abortion	5	0.5%	9	0.9%	5	0.5%	19	0.6%
Education	9	0.9%	7	0.7%	46	4.6%	62	2.1%
Religion	19	2.0%	13	1.3%	7	0.7%	39	1.3%
Law Enforcement	20	2.1%	17	1.7%	25	2.5%	62	2.1%
Corruption	3	0.3%	28	2.8%	15	1.5%	46	1.6%
Individual Crime	25	2.6%	20	2.0%	15	1.5%	60	2.0%
Security	0	0.0%	0	0.0%	0	0.0%	0	0.0%
Disasters	88	9.2%	78	7.8%	77	7.7%	243	8.2%
Accidents	4	0.4%	3	0.3%	14	1.4%	21	0.7%
Deprived Groups	13	1.4%	14	1.4%	13	1.3%	40	1.4%
Human Interest	2	0.2%	5	0.5%	11	1.1%	18	0.6%
Celebrities	5	0.5%	2	0.2%	7	0.7%	14	0.5%
Science	13	1.4%	5	0.5%	14	1.4%	32	1.1%
TV Shows	0	0.0%	4	0.4%	3	0.3%	7	0.2%
Sports	12	1.2%	1	0.1%	11	1.1%	24	0.8%
Baseball	17	1.8%	19	1.9%	17	1.7%	53	1.8%
Basketball	5	0.5%	5	0.5%	5	0.5%	15	0.5%
Football	20	2.1%	0	0.0%	1	0.1%	21	0.7%
Tennis	3	0.3%	5	0.5%	0	0.0%	8	0.3%
Auto Racing	0	0.0%	0	0.0%	0	0.0%	0	0.0%
Golf	7	0.7%	0	0.0%	0	0.0%	7	0.2%
Olympics	0	0.0%	0	0.0%	0	0.0%	0	0.0%
Arts	5	0.5%	3	0.3%	4	0.4%	12	0.4%
Food	9	0.9%	6	0.6%	1	0.1%	16	0.5%
Notices	0	0.0%	0	0.0%	0	0.0%	0	0.0%
Editorials	0	0.0%	0	0.0%	0	0.0%	0	0.0%
Weather	2	0.2%	7	0.7%	7	0.7%	16	0.5%
TOTALS	961	100.0%	996	100.0%	998	100.0%	2,955	100.0%

TABLE 4.6 OCTOBER 1992	ABC	%	CBS	%	NBC	%	TOTAL	%
Govt./Politics	11	1.1%	11	1.2%	11	1.0%	33	1.1%
Elections	24	2.4%	38	4.2%	42	3.9%	104	3.5%
Bush	124	12.4%	123	13.7%	151	14.1%	398	13.4%
Quayle	8	0.8%	10	1.1%	18	1.7%	36	1.2%
Clinton	127	12.7%	96	10.7%	121	11.3%	344	11.6%
Gore	12	1.2%	10	1.1%	20	1.9%	42	1.4%
Perot	57	5.7%	82	9.1%	80	7.5%	219	7.4%
Stockdale	5	0.5%	10	1.1%	5	0.5%	20	0.7%
Families	2	0.2%	1	0.1%	4	0.4%	7	0.2%
Dems	11	1.1%	13	1.4%	13	1.2%	37	1.2%
GOP	15	1.5%	25	2.8%	19	1.8%	59	2.0%
Polls	23	2.3%	17	1.9%	18	1.7%	58	2.0%
Cong. Races	21	2.1%	8	0.9%	18	1.7%	47	1.6%
State & Local	2	0.2%	1	0.1%	15	1.4%	18	0.6%
Media & Politics	13	1.3%	27	3.0%	20	1.9%	60	2.0%
Military	38	3.8%	23	2.6%	39	3.7%	100	3.4%
Army	0	0.0%	0	0.0%	0	0.0%	0	0.0%
Navy	2	0.2%	2	0.2%	4	0.4%	8	0.3%
Air Force	1	0.1%	1	0.1%	1	0.1%	3	0.1%
Marines	0	0.0%	0	0.0%	0	0.0%	0	0.0%
Vets	0	0.0%	0	0.0%	0	0.0%	0	0.0%
Federal Govt.	10	1.0%	2	0.2%	4	0.4%	16	0.5%
State Govt.	4	0.4%	4	0.4%	9	0.8%	17	0.6%
Local Govt.	16	1.6%	11	1.2%	19	1.8%	46	1.5%
International	107	10.7%	52	5.8%	68	6.4%	227	7.6%
Economic Issues	5	0.5%	13	1.4%	15	1.4%	33	1.1%
Status of Economy	42	4.2%	17	1.9%	35	3.3%	94	3.2%
Business	21	2.1%	11	1.2%	20	1.9%	52	1.8%
Labor	12	1.2%	17	1.9%	31	2.9%	60	2.0%
Consumers	1	0.1%	9	1.0%	2	0.2%	12	0.4%
Environment	15	1.5%	5	0.6%	15	1.4%	35	1.2%
Energy	7	0.7%	5	0.6%	0	0.0%	12	0.4%
Transportation	5	0.5%	1	0.1%	12	1.1%	18	0.6%
Health	44	4.4%	59	6.6%	41	3.8%	144	4.8%
Social Issues	2	0.2%	12	1.3%	10	0.9%	24	0.8%
Abortion	2	0.2%	11	1.2%	9	0.8%	22	0.7%
Education	13	1.3%	9	1.0%	11	1.0%	33	1.1%
Religion	10	1.0%	6	0.7%	8	0.7%	24	0.8%
Law Enforcement	22	2.2%	13	1.4%	20	1.9%	55	1.9%
Corruption	24	2.4%	25	2.8%	18	1.7%	67	2.3%
Individual Crime	14	1.4%	10	1.1%	32	3.0%	56	1.9%
Security	0	0.0%	0	0.0%	0	0.0%	0	0.0%
Disasters	11	1.1%	12	1.3%	19	1.8%	42	1.4%
Accidents	16	1.6%	14	1.6%	15	1.4%	45	1.5%
Deprived Groups	22	2.2%	23	2.6%	5	0.5%	50	1.7%
Human Interest	14	1.4%	9	1.0%	12	1.1%	35	1.2%
Celebrities	10	1.0%	4	0.4%	6	0.6%	20	0.7%
Science	15	1.5%	13	1.4%	9	0.8%	37	1.2%
TV Shows	2	0.2%	2	0.2%	0	0.0%	4	0.1%
Sports	5	0.5%	0	0.0%	2	0.2%	7	0.2%
Baseball	13	1.3%	25	2.8%	7	0.7%	45	1.5%
Basketball	1	0.1%	0	0.0%	0	0.0%	1	0.0%
Football	11	1.1%	0	0.0%	4	0.4%	15	0.5%
Tennis	0	0.0%	0	0.0%	0	0.0%	0	0.0%
Auto Racing	0	0.0%	0	0.0%	0	0.0%	0	0.0%
Golf	0	0.0%	0	0.0%	0	0.0%	0	0.0%
Olympics	0	0.0%	0	0.0%	0	0.0%	0	0.0%
Arts	4	0.4%	4	0.4%	1	0.1%	9	0.3%
Food	7	0.7%	1	0.1%	5	0.5%	13	0.4%
Notices	0	0.0%	0	0.0%	0	0.0%	0	0.0%
Editorials	0	0.0%	2	0.2%	0	0.0%	2	0.1%
Weather	0	0.0%	0	0.0%	5	0.5%	5	0.2%
TOTALS	1003	100.0%	899	100.0%	1068	100.0%	2,970	100.0%

director for Bush/Quayle '92, explains that charges of dirty tricks have circulated around Republicans since the time of Richard Nixon. For the Bush campaign, many of the charges stemmed from their use of paid media in 1988 presidential campaign. Matalin suggests that other 1992 candidates such as Perot and Clinton, inoculated themselves from attack journalism simply by claiming that Republicans leaked the information as part of a smear campaign.[6]

List Of 1992 Events That Qualify As Attack Items

July

Bush's "shut up" remark to POW-MIA families
Reports of Bush campaign staff dissention and calls for Bush to quit

Stories about Clinton's alleged marital infidelity
Stories about Clinton's character flaws

Perot's gaffe at an NAACP speech
Reports of Perot's investigations and questionable business practices
Stories about Perot's unpresidential temperament
Reports of staff dissention in Perot's campaign organization

August

Bush's alleged adultery
Reports of Bush campaign dirty tricks
Continued reports of Bush staff dissention and calls for Bush to quit

Stories about Clinton's extra marital affairs
Stories about Clinton's Vietnam Draft status
Stories about Clinton's character flaws

September

Bush's contradictory statements about Iran/Contra

Clinton's Vietnam Draft status

Perot's unpresidential temperament
Perot's investigations and questionable business practices

October

Bush campaign dirty tricks
Bush and Iran/Contra
Iraqgate: Bush administration assistance to Iraq's military build up

Clinton's overseas student demonstrations
Clinton's character flaws
Clinton's Vietnam Draft status

Perot's questionable business practices
Perot's unpresidential temperament

November

Bush and Iran/Contra

Clinton's Vietnam Draft status
Clinton's marital infidelity

Analysis Of Attack Items From Each News Source By Month

July

In July of 1992, attack items made up 30% of the articles about President Bush in *The State,* 44.4% of the Bush items on WIS-TV News, 19.7% on ABC News, 20% on CBS News, and 18.6% on NBC News. As Figure 4.1 shows, the two main topics of attack journalism for Bush in July involved his "shut-up" remark to MIA-POW families. This event led to criticism in the press of unpresidential temperament and compounded news reports of Bush campaign staff turmoil. Bush's POW-MIA controversy made up 33.3% of the Bush items on the WIS local news broadcast in July. This incident of alleged unpresidential temperament ranged from 2.7 to 4% of the total Bush items for July in *The State* and on ABC, CBS, and NBC. News reports of staff dissen-

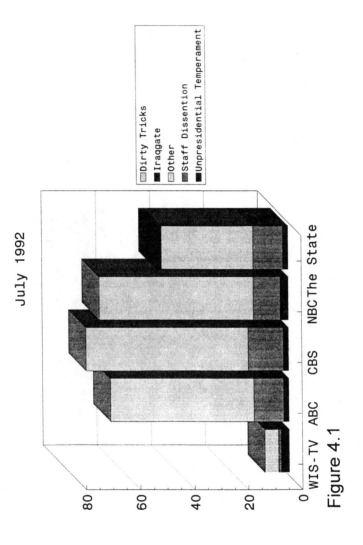

Attack Items - Bush

July 1992

Dirty Tricks
Iraqgate
Other
Staff Dissention
Unpresidential Temperament

WIS-TV   ABC   CBS   NBC The State

Figure 4.1

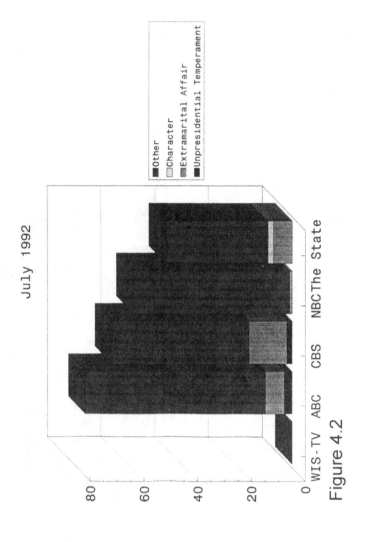

Attack Items - Clinton

July 1992

Figure 4.2

Attack Items - Perot

July 1992

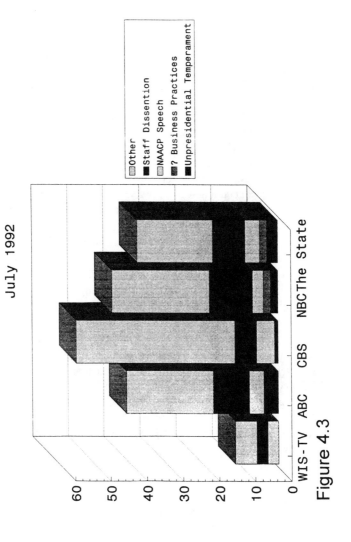

Figure 4.3

Legend:
- Other
- Staff Dissention
- NAACP Speech
- ? Business Practices
- Unpresidential Temperament

Categories: WIS-TV, ABC, CBS, NBC, The State

tion ranged from 11.1% on WIS to 22% of the total Bush articles in July in *The State* newspaper.

As figure 4.2 shows, Clinton had a lower proportion of attack items than Bush in July. Clinton attack stories comprised 19% of the July candidate items in *The State*. Attack items only merited 1.7% of the Clinton coverage on NBC News. Attack news for Clinton was 13% on ABC and 23.9% on CBS. The main issue for Clinton in July involved lingering stories about his alleged extra-marital affairs. For CBS News, the Clinton adultery stories made up 20.9% of the total items in July. Each news source also contained a few items concerning Clinton's unpresidential character.

Ross Perot accumulated the highest percentages of attack items of all three candidates in July. Fifty percent of the Perot coverage on WIS constituted attack news items. Thirty nine percent of the Perot articles in *The State* involved attack stories. Attack items made up 41.3% of the Perot coverage on NBC, 42.9% on ABC, and 21.4% on CBS. As figure 4.3 shows, the attack items for Perot in July fell into four main categories: Perot's gaffe at the NAACP meeting, Perot's unpresidential temperament, Perot's questionable business dealings, and staff dissention in the Perot campaign organization.

The Perot attack items were evenly divided on WIS between reports of staff dissension and the NAACP controversy. Likewise, the disarray in the Perot campaign made up close to 25% of ABC and NBC's coverage of the candidate in July. Problems in the Perot organization fell closer to 10% on CBS and in *The State*. Perot's NAACP remark ranged from 6.5% on NBC News to 10% of the stories in *The State*. There were a few items concerning Perot's questionable business practices on NBC and in *The State* newspaper.

August

In August of 1992, the percentage of attack journalism involving President Bush dropped among all news sources. *The State* had the highest share of Bush attack items at 28%, followed by CBS with 19.8%, WIS with 12.5%, ABC with 9.8%, and NBC with 8.8%. As seen in figure 4.4, the Bush attack items in August fell into four main areas: continued staff dissention in the Bush campaign organization, Republican dirty tricks in the presidential campaign, and allegations that Bush had an extra-marital affair. For Bush, the most damaging media feeding frenzy revolved around the adultery charge. This story

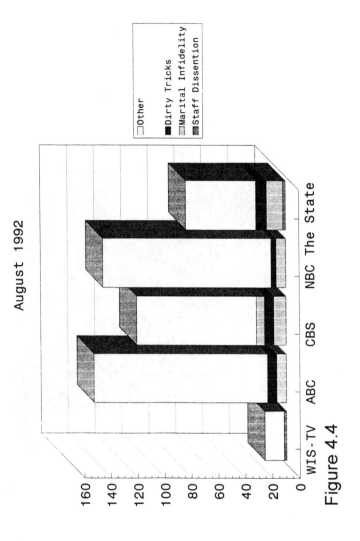

Attack Items - Bush

August 1992

Other
Dirty Tricks
Marital Infidelity
Staff Dissention

WIS-TV   ABC   CBS   NBC   The State

Figure 4.4

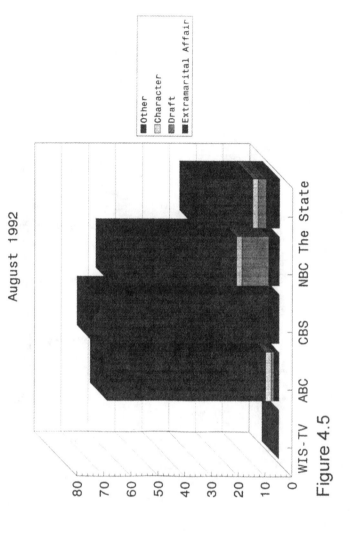

Attack Items - Clinton

August 1992

Figure 4.5

Legend:
- Other
- Character
- Draft
- Extramarital Affair

Y-axis: 0, 10, 20, 30, 40, 50, 60, 70, 80

X-axis: WIS-TV, ABC, CBS, NBC, The State

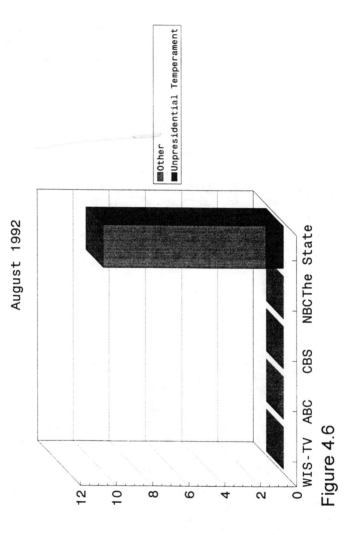

Attack Items - Perot

August 1992

Figure 4.6

received little attention on the local WIS news broadcast. The coverage in the other news sources ranged only from 4.9% to 8.1%, but the Bush adultery story did catalyze the attention of the panelists in this study. The reaction of the panelists to these items will be reported in Chapter 5.

As figure 4.5 shows, the number of attack categories for Clinton expanded to three in August. These items involved continued stories about his alleged adultery, continued reports of his unpresidential character, and stories concerning his Vietnam draft status. *The State* had the highest percentage of Clinton attack items in August with attack journalism making up 32% of the total articles about Governor Clinton. NBC News had the second highest percentage of Clinton attack items at 25.8%. Attack items in the other news sources made up less than 5% of the total Clinton stories. As figure 4.6 demonstrates, Perot, having withdrawn from the race in July, received little media attention and almost no attack stories in August.

September

In September of 1992, attack items in each of the news sources made up less than 16% of the Bush items. The local news sources: *The State* and WIS TV, had a few items concerning Bush campaign dirty tricks. *The State* contained a few residual items about the alleged Bush infidelity. However, as figure 4.7 shows, a new category involving Bush's role in the Iran/Contra affair emerged in the press. In fact, the Iran/Contra stories were the only attack items for Bush on the three network news broadcast in September. ABC News devoted 6.2% of the Bush coverage to Bush's role in the arms for hostage scandal, CBS allocated 10.1%, and NBC allotted 15.7%.

In September, a media feeding frenzy took place involving new allegations about Clinton's Vietnam draft status. As seen in figure 4.8, the local news sources devoted less attention to the matter in comparison to the networks. Fifteen percent of the Clinton stories in *The State* and 13.3% of the Clinton items on WIS News dealt with the draft stories. On NBC, the draft story made up 30.5% of the Clinton items and the Vietnam draft controversy made up 25.3% of the total Clinton items on ABC and CBS. Again, as seen in figure 4.9, Perot, still on hiatus from the campaign, warranted few attack items in September. The networks did run a few stories about his penchant for private investigations and his unpresidential temperament.

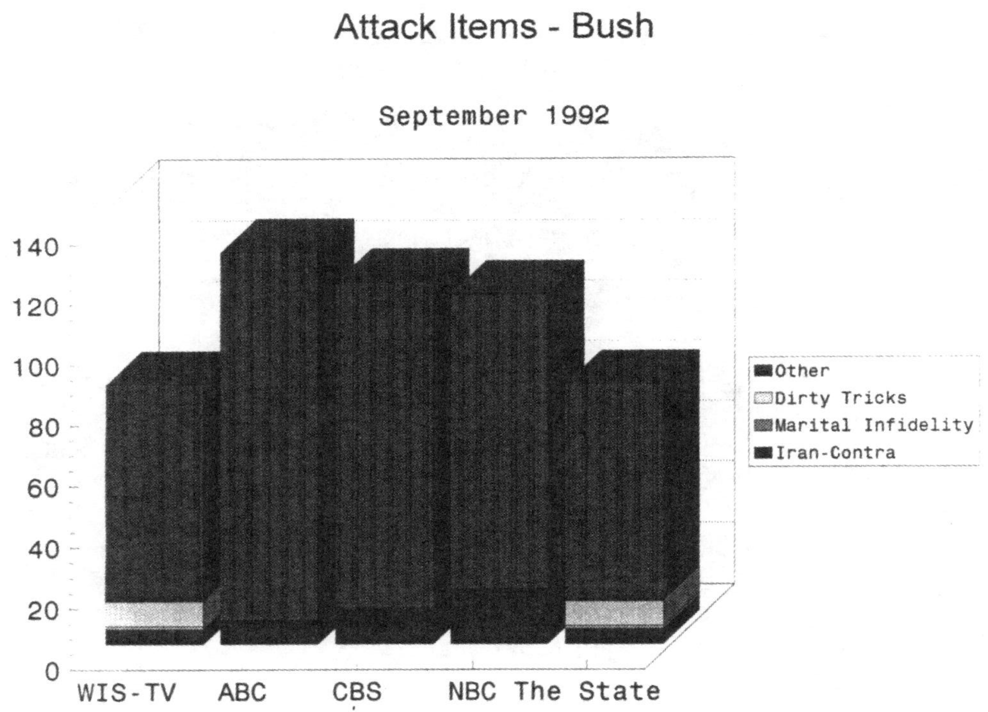
Attack Items - Bush
September 1992
140
120
100
80
60
40
20
0
WIS-TV
ABC
CBS
NBC
The State
Other
Dirty Tricks
Marital Infidelity
Iran-Contra

Figure 4.7

Attack Items - Clinton

September 1992

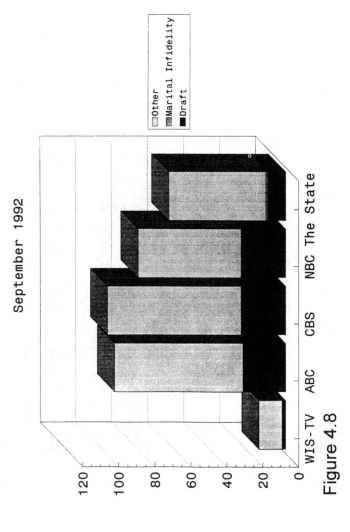

Legend:
- Other
- Marital Infidelity
- Draft

Figure 4.8

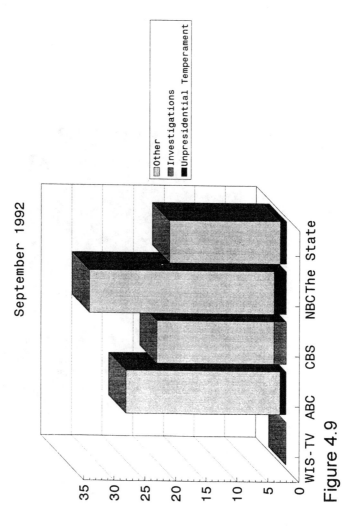

Attack Items - Perot

September 1992

Other
Investigations
Unpresidential Temperament

WIS-TV ABC   CBS   NBC The State

Figure 4.9

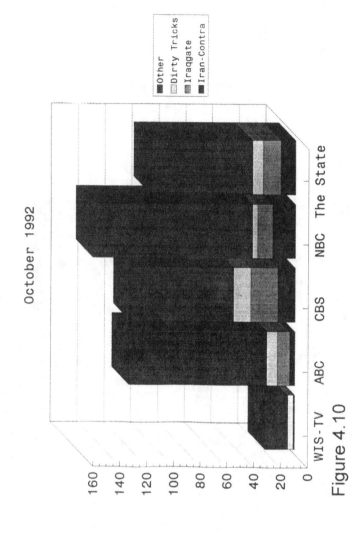

Attack Items - Bush

October 1992

Figure 4.10

Legend:
- Other
- Dirty Tricks
- Iraqgate
- Iran-Contra

Categories: WIS-TV, ABC, CBS, NBC, The State

Scale: 0, 20, 40, 60, 80, 100, 120, 140, 160

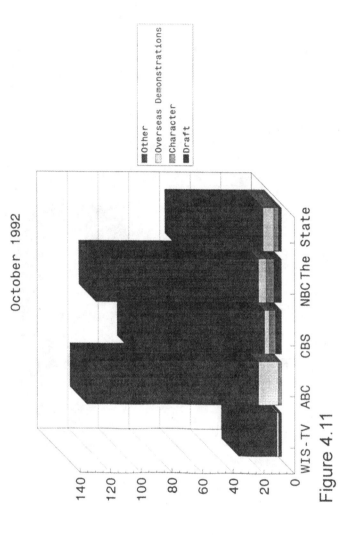

Attack Items - Clinton

October 1992

Figure 4.11

Attack Items - Perot

October 1992

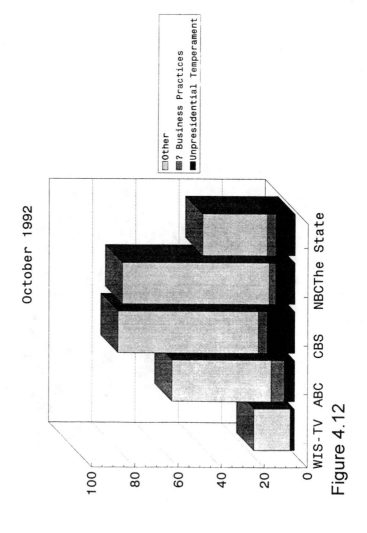

Legend:
- Other
- ? Business Practices
- Unpresidential Temperament

X-axis: WIS-TV ABC CBS NBC The State

Figure 4.12

October

In October of 1992, the share of attack journalism increased for George Bush. As seen in figure 4.10, CBS News had the highest percentage of Bush attack stories at 37.4% followed by *The State* with 26%, WIS News with 22.7%, NBC News with 21.2%, and ABC News with 16.9%. Attack items for Bush in September included increasing reports of dirty tricks on the part of his campaign. For example, the Bush administration illegally leaked information about Clinton's passport files, and Bush began a more aggressive assault on Clinton's character flaws and draft record. Ross Perot alleged that he dropped out of the race, because dirty tricks on the part of the Bush campaign threatened to disrupt his daughter's wedding.

Moreover, in October, continued stories appeared about Bush's involvement in the Iranian arms scandal, and a new charge emerged that the Bush administration was responsible for the military build up of Iraq. The Iraq story merited little coverage on WIS News. "Iraqgate" made up 16.3% of the Bush coverage on CBS, 12% of the articles in *The State,* and 7.3% of the stories on both ABC and NBC.

As figure 4.11 shows, the October attack stories about Clinton were limited to three areas: a few residual stories about his alleged marital infidelity, continued questions about his Vietnam draft status, and a new charge that he led overseas demonstrations while he was a student at Oxford. Overall, *The State* had the highest percentage of Clinton attack items at 19%, followed by NBC at 12.4%, ABC at 11.8%, CBS at 11.5%, and WIS at 10.7%. Perot, now back in the race, generated more news coverage and more attack items. Thirty percent of the October Perot articles in *The State* involved attack stories. Over 20% of the Perot items on CBS news involved attack journalism. Attack stories made up 19.3% of Perot's total on ABC and 15.1% of the total on NBC. WIS News had the lowest percentage of Perot attack items with 10.5%. These Perot attack items involved the familiar areas of unpresidential temperament and questionable business dealings.

November

In the days before the election in November of 1992, Bush received a scattering of attack stories in the newspaper and on the networks involving dirty campaigning and the Iran/Contra affair. Clinton amassed a handful of items on ABC News and in *The State*

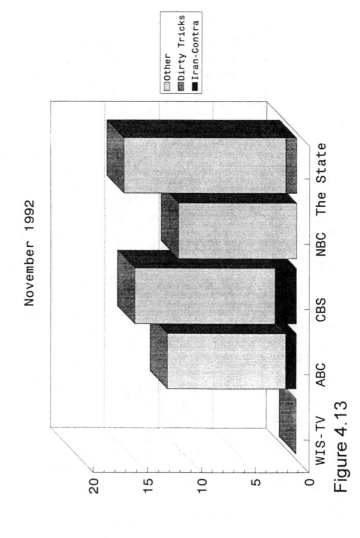

Attack Items - Bush

November 1992

Figure 4.13

Attack Items - Clinton

November 1992

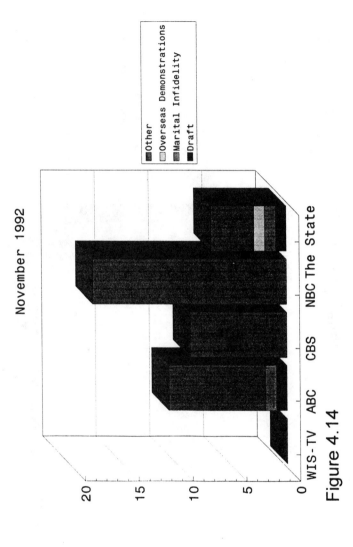

Figure 4.14

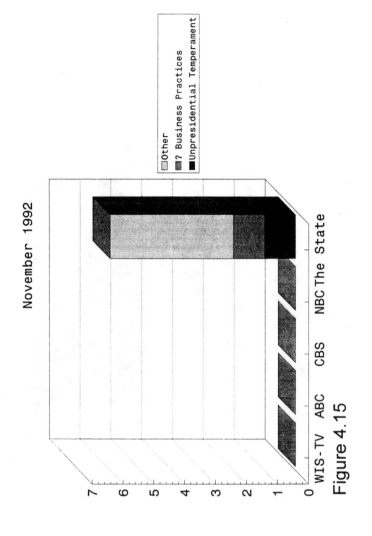

Attack Items - Perot

November 1992

Figure 4.15

reviewing his marital infidelity, Vietnam draft problems, and overseas student demonstrations. Perot generated a couple of items in each of the news sources involving his temperament and business practices. Attack items seemed to disappear on the local WIS News broadcast in the final remaining days of the campaign in November.

Summary Of Attack Item Percentages From Each News Source

Figure 4.16 provides a summary of the attack percentages among all sources for Bush. In general among all sources, the proportion of attack items started relatively high at the start of the campaign, declined after the Republican convention, and rose sharply in October due to the new attack topics of Iraqgate and Iran/Contra. Figure 4.17 shows that the pattern of attacks among all the news sources is less clear for Clinton. In general, the proportion of attacks among all news sources increased significantly during the month of September due to the new reports about Clinton and the Vietnam draft... Figure 4.18 provides a graphic of Perot attack items across all sources. Perot began the campaign with high attack percentages. The attacks declined in August and September after he quit the campaign and increased upon his re-entry in October.

The next chapter will focus on the findings of the panelist interviews. Chapter 5 will highlight each panelist processes election news information with particular emphasis on exposure to attack items.

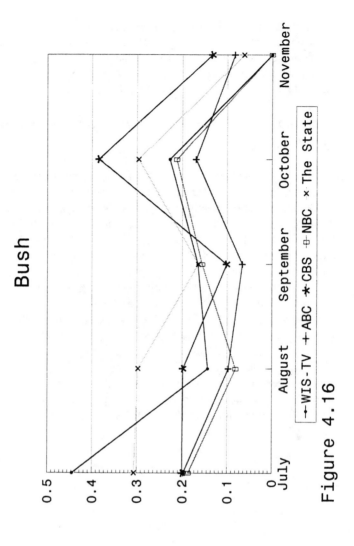

Percentage Attack Items - All Sources

Bush

WIS-TV + ABC ✱ CBS NBC × The State

July   August   September   October   November

Figure 4.16

Percentage Attack Items - All Sources

Clinton

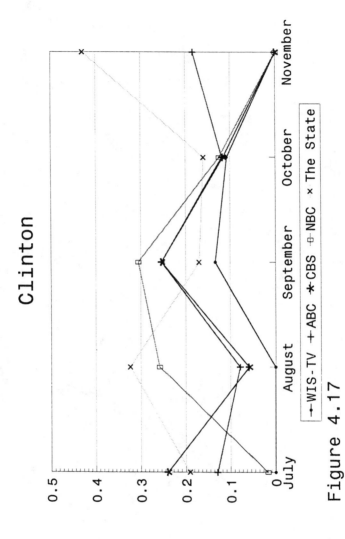

Figure 4.17

Legend: —+— WIS-TV —+— ABC —*— CBS ···□··· NBC ×× The State

Percentage Attack Items - All Sources

Perot

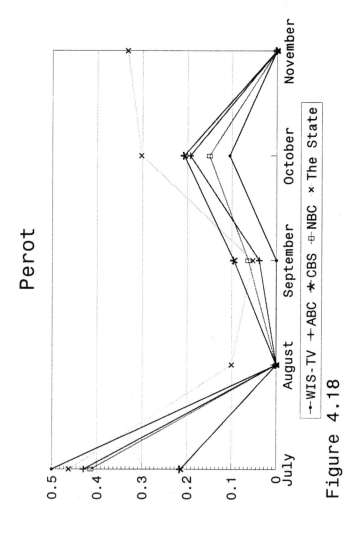

Figure 4.18

Notes:

[1]Staten, Clifford L. and G. Sam Sloss, "The Media and Politics: A Content Analysis of the *Louisville Courier-Journal* during the 1992 Presidential Election," *Journal of Political Science,* Vol. 21, 1993:91-95.

[2]Smith, Ted, J. III, *The Vanishing Economy: Television Coverage of Economic Affairs 1982-1987,* Media Institute, 1988.

[3]Noyes, Richard E., S. Robert Lichter and Daniel R. Amundson, "Was TV Election News Better This Time? A Content Analysis of 1988 and 1992 Campaign Coverage," *Journal of Political Science,* Vol. 21, 1993:16.

[4]Ibid:9.

[5]Sabato, Larry, *Feeding Frenzy: How Attack Journalism Has Transformed American Politics,* 1st edition, The Free Press, 1992:6.

[6]Matalin, Mary and James Carville, *All's Fair: Love, War, and Running For President,* 1st edition, Simon and Schuster, 1994: 7

Chapter 5

Interview Findings

In order to get a better view of voters in the decision-making process and insight into how attack news items affect vote choice, separate interviews were conducted with each of the eighteen panelists. These meetings began immediately after the Democratic Convention in July of 1992 and continued through the first weeks of November of 1992.

Analysts traditionally consider the first days after the Republican convention to be the start of the fall campaign. However, since the renomination of incumbent President George Bush was never seriously in doubt, the assumption in this study was that the 1992 general election campaign would begin earlier than usual, once the Democratic party formally nominated its standard bearer in July.

Interview Procedure

The interview process took place in the following manner. Each panelist was first asked to describe his or her views of Bill Clinton, George Bush and Ross Perot in order to provide a baseline of information for later comparison. Each panelist's impression of the candidates and the 1992 campaign was tracked over time so that, echoing V.O. Key, we can see if the panelists "stand-pat" with their early favorite or "switch" to another candidate later in the campaign. Most importantly, we can see if attack news items affect voter perception of the candidates.

Early Impressions Of The Candidates By Group

Table 5.1: Early Mentions Of Exposure To Attack Items By Group

July	POW-MIA	Bush Staff	Clinton Affairs	Slick Willie	Perot NAACP	Perot Temper	Perot Staff
Group 1							
Carl		X		X		X	X
Ron		X	X	X			X
Bill		X	X		X	X	X
Pete		X	X		X	X	X
Leon		X	X			X	X
Group 2							
Carol		X					X
Marc	X	X	X	X			X
Charles		X		X			X
Maggie		X		X			X
Hilda		X	X			X	X
Group 3							
Penny		X		X		X	X
Craig		X		X			X
Elaine		X			X	X	X
Bill		X		X			X
Group 4							
Darlene		X		X		X	X
Deidre		X	X	X		X	X
Sandra		X		X		X	X
Bettie							

1. High Political Interest/Easy Media Access

Before the start of the 1992 general election campaign, members of the high political interest/easy media access group expressed interest in different candidates. Carl Adams was the only member of the first group who supported President Bush's re-election in his initial questionnaire. Pete Diedrich selected Bill Clinton. Leon Evans was undecided. Ronald Burton and Bill Creighton were early Perot backers.

Group #1 Views of George Bush

As Table 5.1 shows, all five members of the first group were aware of the reports of staff turmoil in the Bush/Quayle '92 campaign organization. Even the lone Bush supporter in the group, Carl Adams, acknowledged that the President and his campaign had shortcomings, but Adams blamed most of Bush's problems on the Democrats in Congress. Bill Creighton was especially condemning of Bush. Creighton's main complaint was Bush's inconsistent economic philosophy:

> You can't go 180 degrees as he did on an economic policy. From being totally washed out, negative on Mr. Reagan's economic policy and coining the phrase "voodoo economics" and when somebody nominates him as Vice President, saying he's seen the light. That's too wishy-washy for me.[1]

However, three of the five members of the first group: Bill Creighton, Pete Diedrich, and Leon Evans, were able to disagree with President Bush on issues, but still like him as a person. As Leon Evans stated, "George Bush is a likeable person and his wife is one of the best First Ladies we've ever had."[2]

Ronald Burton's views on George Bush as a person differed from the other members of the first group. Burton expressed a much more negative view of the President at the start of the general election:

> I think George Bush has a very shady past. I think that, ah, I've watched him for a number of years. I thought, at first, in the late '80s he would make a good president. He's been very ineffectual and he's just ignored the plight of the common working person. He's turned a lot of attention to some very wealthy people. His Club 100 or so. The people who've contributed at least 100,000 a year in soft money that gets cycled back into his campaign.[3]

Similarly, two members of the high political interest/easy media access group: Ronald Burton and Pete Diedrich described Bush as wealthy during their initial interviews. Diedrich thought that Bush's isolation from the common people was due to his race and higher socioeconomic status:

> I think the President is a good man, but I think he's out of touch. I think the President, through no fault of his, has been in the privileged

group of Americans. He is a white American male that was born very well off. He is associated in the right circles. He really has a belief that things are going well. He has a belief that there is a certain role for women to play, for minorities to play, a certain role for youth to play, and there's a certain role for the have nots to play. And to keep those in kilter, you keep the white American male at the top making the decisions and being able to manipulate the public relations such that everyone feels that they're doing well. I think he's out of touch.[4]

Group #1 Views of Bill Clinton

As seen in Table 5.1, the attack news items involving Bill Clinton's alleged adultery clearly affected four out of the five members of the high political interest/easy media access group. However, Bill Creighton, Pete Diedrich, and Leon Evans all felt that the issue would not hurt Clinton's electability. In fact, Creighton surprisingly suggested that Clinton's ability to survive media attacks would actually help him govern the country better:

> You have got to, really, with all the backbiting today and all the research that goes into background, be a person that has the type of resiliency that I think he has shown. Right now with all the urban problems, economic problems, world problems, it's going to take someone with that kind of resiliency, who can take the basting to make the tough decisions.[5]

Ronald Burton again argued the opposite point of view and specifically cited the adultery stories as a main reason why he did not trust Clinton:

> I think the problems with his different extra-marital affairs that have been publicized. He's, uh, if he can't make a promise on a wedding vow or whatever, then you really won't uphold your oath of office.[6]

Likewise, Burton also had the most negative evaluation of Clinton based on media reports about his record as Governor of Arkansas:

> He's had a number of problems in Arkansas. His economy is not doing very well. He's had problems with his social welfare agencies and taking care of, basically, indigent children that have fallen into foster care. He's ignored those problems.[7]

Attack news items involving Clinton's character and trustability were first mentioned in the high political interest/easy media access group by Carl Adams and Ronald Burton. In his explanation as to why he did not trust Clinton, Carl Adams also made reference to Clinton's admission of past use of drugs:

> I don't trust him, because of his evasiveness about things that he's done. Questions that are asked of him, he would evade the question. He would give a long rambling non-answer, very much like Perot. Not as bad as Perot, but he wouldn't really answer. He would evade and give a technically correct answer, but not be 100% truthful. For example, there was the dope smoking episode. That's not a big deal, but I think it showed a lack of character or candor. I think he should have said, "Yeah, I smoked dope a couple times, big deal."[8]

Leon Evans and Pete Diedrich were the most positive in the first group about Clinton's record and issue stances. Evans even raised Clinton to the lofty level of Democratic President Franklin Delano Roosevelt: "Clinton's the only one who has a plan, but I don't know if he can go into detail. He needs time like FDR."[9] Diedrich, also impressed with Clinton's record and issue stances, commented:

> I would look at Bill's record. I'd look at a poor boy coming up in Arkansas and I believe going to Yale. Ah, overseas, I believe, he was a Rhodes Scholar. I would look at what he's attempted to do in a poor Southern state. I would look at his stance on education, because in a democracy, education is key.[10]

Only one member of the high political interest/easy media access group, Leon Evans, mentioned Clinton's selection of Gore as an important campaign development. Similarly, Carl Adams was the only member of the first group who mentioned Clinton's Democratic Party affiliation in his early description of the candidates. Adams was somewhat positive about Clinton's attempts to change the Democratic platform to a more mainstream stance.

Group #1 Views of Ross Perot

Table 5.1 also shows that although they were intrigued by the prospect of a third party candidacy, all the panelists in the first group except Ron Burton expressed a measure of uncertainty about Ross

Perot's temperament. The commentary of Carl Adams sums up these concerns:

> So many people are just fed up with the way the system is, Repub-
> lican and Democratic, that they thought this was a chance to just
> shake the system down and, you know, really make a difference. Um,
> as it turns out, him being a non-politician, uh, I think he was
> beginning to turn a lot of people off. Because to be a president, I
> think, you have to be a politician. You have to be tactful, I mean,
> there's a lot to it. More than say, being a good businessman.[11]

Two of the five panelists from the high interest/easy access group: Bill Creighton and Pete Diedrich, recounted Perot's widely reported gaffe at the NAACP. Perot's mistake highlighted his behavioral problems. As Mr. Diedrich explained:

> You see, in this real media electronic age, you gotta make sure you
> say things the right way because you can't take them back. With his
> speech to the NAACP, personally I wouldn't have made that much of
> a to do about it, but, when you're talking to black folk you never say:
> "you people." We've been "you peopled" too long. Ross was sincere
> when he said that, but he didn't realize how it would come over. If he
> had listened to his advisers, they'd say: "When your speaking to
> black folk you don't do that or some of my best friends were black or
> when Aunt Jane worked in my kitchen." If you want to turn off - he
> didn't mean any harm, he, that's the way he saw things. He also,
> because of his success he feels his word is the last word. You can't
> do that with this country.[12]

Each member of the first group made mention of the staff problems in the Perot campaign organization and all were aware of his unexpected withdrawal from the presidential election. Of all the members in this first group, Ronald Burton was the most shocked and disappointed by Perot's announcement to suspend his campaign.

2. High Political Interest/Difficult Media Access Group

At the early stages of the 1992 presidential campaign, members of the high political interest/difficult media access group were divided between support for Ross Perot and uncertainty. Three of the panelists from the high interest/difficult access group: Carol Bach, Marc

Jackman, and Charles Ippolitos, expressed support for Ross Perot in their initial questionnaires. The remaining two members of this group: Maggie Gaylord and Hilda Holmquist indicated that they were undecided about the 1992 contest.

Group #2 Views of George Bush

Again, as Table 5.1 demonstrates, each of the five members of the second group knew about the turbulence in the Bush campaign organization. Also, four of the five panelists in the second group: Carol Bach, Marc Jackman, Maggie Gaylord, and Hilda Holmquist had an unfavorable impression of Bush as a person. Maggie Gaylord expressed the strongest disliking of the President, calling him "a no good, no count, branch on a tree."[13] Marc Jackman was quite disturbed by Bush's remarks to the POW-MIA families. Jackman described Bush as being out of synch with average Americans:

> He's part of the established elite who are out of touch with the average citizen. But Bush is Presidential and I admire his handling of the Persian Gulf War. Still, he is too removed from the problems of the everyday person. I feel he talks down to us on TV and his personality is somewhat cocky.[14]

Likewise, Hilda Holmquist expressed a distaste for both President Bush and Vice President Quayle:

> Bush and Quayle still haven't heard what people are saying. Still aren't tuned into what, I think, are some of the issues and concerns that people may have. I'm operating from a fundamental principle that anybody, Donald Duck, would be better than George Bush and Dan Quayle. I mean, clearly. I think, first of all, I'm troubled by the fact that Dan Quayle is a heartbeat away from the presidency. I think he lacks intelligence, judgement, experience. I don't think four years with George Bush has helped him any.[15]

Of all five members of the second group, Charles Ippolitos was the most positive about Bush and, like Marc Jackman, made an effort to point out his foreign policy achievements. However, Maggie Gaylord's views clashed with her fellow panelist from the high interest/difficult access group on Bush's foreign policy record:

Mr. Bush, to me, has done absolutely nothing for the American people, especially the homeless and, ah, getting them out of the parks and getting them into a home. But yet he can go abroad to Russia and different foreign countries and, and give out and hand out free-all. Where our tax dollars as American citizens, I feel like, should go towards our American citizens.[16]

Group #2 Views of Bill Clinton

As shown in Table 5.1, two of the five panelists from the high political interest/difficult media access group: Marc Jackman and Hilda Holmquist, mentioned attack news items about Clinton's alleged adultery in their first interviews. Hilda Holmquist suggested that the timing of the stories may have helped some panelists cope with the reports of Clinton's marital infidelity:

Bill Clinton has been a surprise for being able to get through, oh, some of the seamy side of the media and emerge with credibility. Part of it was luck. I think if the Gennifer Flowers thing had come out in mid-October, it would have killed him. But it came out early, and if there was an opportunity to do damage control, it would be early in a race, not late in a race. So I think timing helped him. I think he had the guts to stick it out. I don't think people see that it probably didn't matter anyway. After a while it was like, so what? It lost its scandal value and I think he had shown on the fundamental question of "did he or didn't he?," he hedged on it consistently enough that people just gave up on it.[17]

Charles Ippolitos liked Clinton's policy ideas, but was skeptical about his ability to finance them. Similarly, Carol Bach had a lukewarm reaction to Clinton at the start of the general election, but seemed drawn to his position on economic issues:

I'm not that excited about Clinton, but at least he is thinking about the economy. There is a question of realistic vision. Clinton seems to have a more realistic vision of the economic situation. [18]

Even though the news content analysis in July revealed only a tiny fraction of stories about the wives of the presidential candidates, one member of the high political interest/difficult media access group, Maggie Gaylord, formulated a poor impression of Governor Clinton, because of her perception of Hillary's strong influence:

I think I would say that Bill Clinton is pushed and motivated by Mrs. Clinton and that, ah, if he becomes president, he will not be president; Mrs. Clinton will be president. [19]

Three of the five members of the high political interest/difficult media access group: Carol Bach, Charles Ippolitos, and Maggie Gaylord, also had a strong reaction to Clinton's selection of Senator Al Gore for Vice President. Bach and Ippolitos were generally positive about the addition of Gore to the Democratic ticket, but Maggie Gaylord said the Gore selection made her feel worse about Clinton:

> The selection of Gore made me feel a little worse about him. The two of them, to me, are no better than Bush and Quayle. Basically, because, I don't know that much about Gore, but what I've heard of him, ah, he, from what I've gathered from talking to different people, he is, basically, how do I say it? He basically, whether he is in the Vice Presidency race or not, his views may be close to Bill Clinton's, but there is just something about the man and his character that makes me wary, very wary. [20]

Group #2 Views of Ross Perot

Table 5.1 shows that all the members of the second group had heard reports that Ross Perot's campaign was coming apart before he quit the race. They were also disappointed with the candidate himself, because of his lack of specificity on the issues. Hilda Holmquist's comments sum up the frustration of this second group regarding Perot's issues stances:

> Perot was the surprise in terms of injecting himself into the process, looking real, real good at the front end, but as he went along, kind of, I don't know, just not producing. OK? He kind of had a lot of good rhetoric at the front end, but not backed up and I think the primary issue being the inability to state a position and to articulate a position about what he was doing. He had a lot of simplistic solutions to complex problems. [21]

However, one member of the group was deeply troubled by Perot's early exit from the campaign. As Charles Ippolitos stated:

> Until Perot came along, I was a Republican. Now I'm an independent and I'm disappointed that he won't run. I thought he provided an

alternative. He said things people wanted to hear and people were surprised by that. People are tired of business as usual and the two party system. Now it looks like we're back to that. [22]

3. Low Political Interest/Easy Media Access Group

Members of the low political interest/easy access group were split as to which candidate to support before the start of the general election. Penny Lobmon selected George Bush in her initial questionnaire. Elaine Miller expressed support for Arkansas Governor Bill Clinton. Bill Nystrum favored Ross Perot and Craig Koll was undecided early in the 1992 campaign.

Group #3 Views of George Bush

As seen from Table 5.1, all four panelists in the third group were aware that the Bush campaign was in trouble in the early stages of the 1992 general election. Penny Lobmon and Craig Koll stated that President Bush's record and poor job performance were the cause of his campaign difficulties. For example, Koll said that Bush's inconsistent issue stances might cause his defeat at the polls:

> But, ah, seems to be the biggest problem with Bush is he, if he had never said that no more new taxes, I think he'd have been a lot better off. But, ah, I don't think he's going to make it this time. [23]

Two of the four panelists in the third group, Elaine Miller and Bill Nystrum, specifically mentioned George Bush's past work as Director of the Central Intelligence Agency as a reason for disliking him. As Elaine stated:

> Bush is the former head of the CIA. I mean, give me a break. Who is he kidding? Who in their right mind would know that and vote for him? I'm astounded, I mean, I know it sounds really gauche to refer to cloak and dagger stuff, but, I've never been a big James Bond fan, but, I mean, that stuff goes on. More and more is being revealed about things that went on while Bush was head of the CIA. I can't support someone who engages in that type of conduct. [24]

Group 3 Views of Clinton

One member of group three, Elaine Miller, claimed that Bill Clinton's general physical attractiveness helped him to overcome the media attacks such as the controversy that erupted concerning his past drug experimentation:

> I think a lot of his success has to do with his looks. I mean his got that John Kennedy veneer. Even though he had some blemishes like that stuff about he didn't inhale, but I think people are probably ready for a younger more down to earth person who can share more common experiences with the voters. Things cycle and its about time for the Democrats. Plus, he kind of has that golden boy appeal and for that reason I haven't been paying a whole lot of attention to what he's been saying. I'm watching what's happening around him and how the public is reacting to him. [25]

Two of the four panelists in the third group: Elaine Miller and Bill Nystrum, cited Clinton's Democratic Party affiliation in their early views of his candidacy. In fact, Nystrum placed his entire evaluation of Clinton in terms of a political party context:

> This is going to sound extremely negative and cynical, but he is a man who has several virtues. One of them is that the party heads think they can control him and the other one is that they think he has a chance to win. I don't think he's a bad guy, but even if he wins, I don't think he's going to make any impact that I can see. I don't think the party heads would pick someone who wasn't easily controlled. [26]

Group 3 Views of Perot

Three of the four panelists from the low interest/easy access group: Penny Lobmon, Craig Koll, and Elaine Miller, mentioned Perot's status as a wealthy business executive in their initial interviews. News reports of Perot's questionable business dealings and unpresidential behavior actually frightened Penny Lobmon: "Ross Perot scared me really. The thought of him getting into office scared me to death." [27]

Likewise, Elaine Miller also mentioned Perot's problematic speech to the NAACP convention as an example of his unpresidential behavior. Table 5.1 clearly demonstrates that each of the members of group four knew about the staff dissention in Perot's campaign organization.

Thus it is no surprise that no one in the group seemed astonished by Perot's withdrawal from the 1992 contest.

4. Low Political Interest/Difficult Media Access Group

Three of the four members of the low political interest/difficult media access group: Darlene Ross, Deidre Utley, and Bettie Tisdale supported George Bush in their initial questionnaires. The fourth member of the group, Sandra Sandelius, voted for George Bush in 1988, but remained uncommitted at the early stages of the 1992 general election.

Group 4 Views of Bush

The low interest /difficult access group was unanimous in the opinion that George Bush is a "good person." However, as seen in Table 5.1, three of the four members knew about the reports of internal difficulties in the Bush campaign organization. These same three panelists also expressed concerns about Bush's performance in office. Darlene Ross connected Bush's wealthy economic status to his Republican party affiliation. As Ross concisely stated, "Bush is a Republican. The Republicans are more for the rich people."[28]

Bettie Tisdale was the only person from the low interest/difficult access group who spoke positively about Bush in terms of his record on economic matters:

> I think he means well and, um, he wants to do all the things that is necessary for the people to get by and help them get jobs and stuff like that. I believe, you know, he's able to do all the things he says he can do. I think he should be President again, yeah. In my opinion, he ought to be President again.[29]

Group 4 Views of Clinton

As Table 5.1 shows, only one member of group four, Deidre Utley, expressed strong negative reactions toward Clinton based on attack news items about his alleged adultery. Sandra Sandelius, like

Elaine Miller from group three, explained that Bill Clinton's success in the presidential primaries was due to his good looks: "Bill Clinton got the Democratic nomination. He, in a certain way, is attractive. In the U.S. candidacies you always see the nice looking guy with the nomination."[30]

Three of the four panelists from the low political interest/difficult media access group: .Darlene Ross, Deidre Utley, and Sandra Sandelius highlighted Clinton's Democratic Party affiliation in their early descriptions of him. Darlene Ross was the most negative among the group: "Clinton is a Democrat, who I believe is another Jimmy Carter."[31]

Darlene Ross and Deidre Utley both mentioned Clinton's selection of Al Gore in their early interviews. Utley made a special note of Gore's appearance: "Clinton is running on the Democratic ticket and he's chosen a good looking running partner in Gore."[32] Finally, Sandra Sandelius described Clinton "as a nice guy," but more interested in domestic policies than in the foreign affairs.[33]

Group 4 Views of Perot

Three of the four panelists from the low political interest/difficult media access group: Darlene Ross, Deidre Utley and Sandra Sandelius, made note of Perot's status as a wealthy businessman Sandelius specifically mentioned attack news items concerning Perot's questionable business dealings:

> Being a millionaire and being so first in some areas, people accused him of doing quote "wrong things." Well, it was reported in *Time* that he was working for IBM, he did several things. Getting the commission from IBM and then the sales were cancelled. It didn't surprise me. I thought that from the beginning, given his background that something would be coming out, the other shoe, you know.[34]

One panelist from the fourth group, Deidre Utley, made mention of Perot's independent party affiliation. Darlene Ross stated that she did not like Perot, because of his unpresidential demeanor. As seen in Table 5.1, only Bettie Tisdale from the low interest/difficult access group could not identify Ross Perot and did not remark about his withdrawal announcement.

Panelist Reaction To The Democratic Convention

The Democratic convention helped to generate more news coverage of Bill Clinton. The news content analysis in Chapter 4 shows that the volume of news items about Clinton nearly equalled the number of Bush items in each of the news sources during the month of July. Thus, it is important to gauge the exposure of the panelists to this event since Democratic campaign strategists had attempted to limit the cumulative damage of the media attacks on Clinton from the primaries by trying to "re-invent" his image during the Democratic National Convention.

Table 5.2: Panelist exposure to the Democratic National Convention

	Watched All	*Watched Some*	*Did Not Follow*
Group One			
Carl Adams	X		
Ron Burton	X		
Bill Creighton		X	
Pete Diedrich	X		
Leon Evans	X		
Group 2			
Carol Bach		X	
Marc Jackman		X	
Charles Ippolitos	X		
Maggie Gaylord			X
Hilda Holmquist	X		
Group 3			
Penny Lobmon		X	
Craig Koll		X	
Elaine Miller	X		
Bill Nystrum		X	
Group 4			
Darlene Ross		X	
Deidre Utley		X	
Sandra Sandelius			X
Bettie Tisdale		X	

The Democratic Convention dominated network primetime and many cable stations. Hence, for anyone watching evening television, it was difficult to avoid. As Table 5.2 shows, all of the panelists, except Maggie Gaylord of the high interest/difficult access group and Sandra Sandelius from the low interest/difficult access group, had at least some exposure to the Democratic convention. Maggie Gaylord, who described herself as an avid reader of novels and historical works, read books during the nights of televised convention coverage. Sandra Sandelius said she was too busy studying at night during the coverage.

As one might expect, panelists in both high political interest groups followed the convention fairly regularly, each night it was shown. Panelists from the high political interest/difficult media access group gave two explanations for why they had increased viewership of this political event. Those with heavy work schedules or young children typically missed the regularly scheduled early evening news on any given day. However, the media coverage of the convention occurred during primetime after work, which gave these panelists unique media access. Moreover, the convention was a special event which captured their interest and caused them to set aside time to follow the coverage.

Of the sixteen panelists who watched television coverage of the Democratic Convention, the majority could not recall exactly which station they settled on to watch convention. The panelists in the low political interest groups begrudgingly followed the convention as there seemed to them that there was nothing else to watch on television that week. These panelists watched sporadically and flipped from station to station.

However, four of the eighteen panelists followed the convention loyally on specific channels. For example, Hilda Holmquist selected public television and NBC, because they worked out a special arrangement for joint coverage. Both Leon Evans and Bill Nystrum specifically chose to watch the convention on C-SPAN so they could watch it without the television commentators. Marc Jackman followed the convention loyally on CNN and commented that the Democrats seemed to had their act together this time.

Reaction To The Bush Adultery Stories

Panelist reactions to the Bush adultery stories which appeared in the media before the Republican Convention during the second week of August, support my hypothesis that "attack stories" involving character issues tend to catalyze the attention of voters regardless of political interest and media access. As Table 5.3 clearly demonstrates, only one panelist, Bill Nystrum of the low political interest/easy media access group, was not aware of the allegations of adultery that engulfed the Bush campaign immediately preceding the Republican National Convention.

Table 5.3: Panelist exposure to news reports of Bush's alleged affair

Group 1	Mentioned Bush Adultery Story	No Mention of Bush Adultery Story
Carl Adams	X	
Ron Burton	X	
Bill Creighton	X	
Pete Diedrich	X	
Leon Evans	X	
Group 2		
Carol Bach	X	
Marc Jackman	X	
Charles Ippolitos	X	
Maggie Gaylord	X	
Hilda Holmquist	X	
Group 3		
Penny Lobmon	X	
Craig Koll	X	
Elaine Miller	X	
Bill Nystrum		X
Group 4		
Darlene Ross	X	
Deidre Utley	X	
Sandra Sandelius	X	
Bettie Tisdale	X	

The two most detailed recollections of the incident were given by panelists Carol Bach and Charles Ippolitos from the high political interest/difficult media access group. Bach recalled stories about Bush affairs dating back to the 1988 campaign: "I had heard rumors about Bush's infidelity when he ran against Dukakis. So, this has not been that new to me. I think the fact that the campaign has not mentioned Clinton's transgressions bears out the truth of the rumor."[35] Ippolitos, who voted for Bush in 1988 and was an early Perot supporter in the 1992 campaign, recalled watching the President's interview with Stone Phillips on *Dateline NBC* on August 11th:

> I'm remembering in just catching up a little bit about charges of sleaze and dirty campaigning and things like that. I do recall a television show where the President was asked whether he had an affair and that's where he basically referred to it as perpetuating this sleaze. I think that's the first time I had actually heard that. Although there may have been one other time when somebody on the Republican National Committee had made a statement where he disagreed with it and said he didn't approve of this kind of sleaze.[36]

The reaction of panelists who supported Bush to the media coverage of the adultery charges is informative in terms of cognitive information processing of attack journalism. Panelists like Deidre Utley from the low political interest/difficult media access group, who said she would withhold support for Clinton because cheated on his wife, seemed to have a double standard when similar charges were lodged against President Bush. Utley simply dismissed the Bush adultery stories as "Bah humbug."[37]

Three other Bush supporters: Penny Lobmon, Darlene Ross, and Bettie Tisdale, also mentioned that they had heard about the adultery charges, but did not believe them. As Tisdale, a member of the low political interest/difficult media access group, stated, "Who is sleeping with who. I'm not concerned about that. They should leave the man alone. Let him do his job. We should be concerned with all them teenage girls having babies."[38]

The Clinton supporters were more consistent with their beliefs about the relevance of private personal matters in political elections. For example, Pete Diedrich of the high political interest/easy media access group commented, "I don't pay that much attention to that stuff, whether it is George Bush or Bill Clinton. All those things are smoke screens to cover up the issues. There are very few men who some woman can't stand up and say something about. I don't condone that sort of thing, but I'm not concerned about that."[39] Elaine Miller from the low political interest/easy media access group was also critical of the injection of adultery as a campaign issue, but she criticized Bush's response to the allegations:

> All this mud going back and forth about affairs. I just want to tell them to grow up. But I did think Bush's response to that was absolutely absurd. I can't believe he thinks the American public don't see that first he irately tells the press that they're into sleaze and then they turn around and his campaign people say that this is an important issue that has to be addressed by the Clinton campaign. I mean, that is the height of hypocrisy.[40]

Panelist Reaction To The Republican Convention

Like the Democratic National Convention, the Republican National Convention dominated network primetime as well as several cable stations. However most political analysts reached a consensus that the Republican event generated a negative backlash among voters due to the strident tone of the convention. As with the Democratic Convention, panelists in this study with high political interest tended to follow the Republican Convention with regularity regardless of media access difficulties. The panelists with low political interest tended to follow sporadically and somewhat against their will since there was little else to watch on network television.

Table 5.4: Panelist exposure to the Republican National Convention

	Watched All	Watched Some	Did Not Follow
Group 1			
Carl Adams	X		
Ron Burton	X		
Bill Creighton		X	
Pete Diedrich	X		
Leon Evans	X		

Group 2

Carol Bach	X	
Marc Jackman	X	
Charles Ippolitos	X	
Maggie Gaylord		X
Hilda Holmquist (X)		

Group 3

Penny Lobmon	X
Craig Koll	X
Elaine Miller	X
Bill Nystrum	X

Group 4

Darlene Ross	X	
Deidre Utley	X	
Sandra Sandelius		X
Bettie Tisdale	X	

Once again, as seen in Table 5.4, Maggie Gaylord and Sandra Sandelius were the only panelists who did not follow the Republican National Convention. As Maggie commented, "No I didn't watch it. Ah, I didn't watch it, because they lie. All of them say: "read my lips." You better be thinking for yourself. Read his lips, if you want to. Not me."[41] However, unlike the reactions to the Democratic Convention, many of the panelists were either disappointed or openly critical of the Republican Convention's proceedings.

For example, Darlene Ross, a panelist from the low political interest/difficult media access group, unhappily followed the Republican convention in a piecemeal fashion while searching for something else to watch. The overall tone of the convention disturbed Darlene: "I didn't like all the talk about abortion. I'm a Republican, but I'm pro-choice.[42] Likewise, Marc Jackman, from the high political interest/difficult media access group, who again followed only CNN's convention coverage, commented: "The Republicans let the right wing run things this time."[43] Leon Evans from the high political interest/easy media access group agreed:

> They let the extremists take over the whole thing. I watched the whole convention and I didn't hear anything about what Bush is

going to do about the deficit or, ah, doing something about the
economy. I think, let's see, ah, Barbara Bush made the best speech.
The others were just screaming and yelling like children.[44]

Bill Nystrum from the low interest/easy media access group
mentioned that Bush's inability to handle the economy and his promise
at the convention to utilize James Baker for domestic priorities showed
his "lack of fitness for office."[45]

For the panelists who followed the Republican convention, the
most memorable episode was former President Reagan's address to the
delegates. As Carol Bach from the high political interest/difficult media
access group commented:

> I valiantly tried watching the Republican Convention, but I tended to
> fall asleep. The night of Reagan's speech was very disheartening.
> How all those people could admire one of the most corrupt, inept
> presidents in our time — I'll never understand. Even Nixon has the
> saving grace of a brilliant political instinct, although he's corrupt as
> well.[46]

Bettie Tisdale from the low political interest/difficult media access
group also mentioned Reagan's speech: "I had the TV on, but I was in
and out. There was nothing else to watch, but I did see President
Reagan. He's like a granddaddy to me."[47] Charles Ippolitos, another
member of group two said, "I listened to part of it, but yet, I even, ah,
dozed off to sleep before Ronnie started, OK? But I just haven't held
the interest for some reason and I can't explain it."[48]

Panelists Re-examine Clinton's Draft Status

After the Republican convention, a media feeding frenzy involving
Clinton's Vietnam Draft question emerged in the press. New allegations arose questioning whether or not Clinton's uncle had pulled
strings with elected officials in order to block Bill Clinton's entry into
the draft lottery. The news content analysis in Chapter 4 shows that this
story made up the largest share of Clinton's attack items during the
month of September, 1992.

Table 5.5: Panelist exposure to the Clinton Vietnam Draft story

	Mentioned Clinton Vietnam Draft Story	No Mention of Clinton Vietnam Draft Story
Group 1		
Carl Adams	X	
Ron Burton	X	
Bill Creighton	X	
Pete Diedrich	X	
Leon Evans	X	
Group 2		
Carol Bach	X	
Marc Jackman	X	
Charles Ippolitos	X	
Maggie Gaylord	X	
Hilda Holmquist	X	
Group 3		
Penny Lobmon	X	
Craig Koll	X	
Elaine Miller	X	
Bill Nystrum	X	
Group 4		
Darlene Ross	X	
Deidre Utley	X	
Sandra Sandelius	X	
Bettie Tisdale		X

The draft story had followed Clinton since the New Hampshire primary and each of the panelists in this study had periodically expressed their thoughts on the matter over the course of the campaign. As Table 5.5 shows, only Bettie Tisdale from the low political interest/difficult media access group failed to mention the new allegations concerning Clinton's draft status that flooded the press in September 1992.

The most forgiving of Clinton's actions were three panelists close to Clinton's age. Carol Bach's comments were typical of this group:

"Having grown up with Vietnam, watching classmates registering for the draft at the end of the war, I have no problem with anyone wanting to avoid that war."[49]

Elaine Miller said, "I was 18 during the final year of the draft lotteries and my finance was 19. It was very scary. I can understand what Clinton was going through."[50] Similarly, Charles Ippolitos stated:

> If I go back to that time period and remember things that were going on at that time. It was a pretty large group that was doing the same kind of thing. It wasn't like we were talking about two or three individuals who were doing this. Guys were leaving to go to Canada, OK? Many people were signing up for the National Guard or the Air National Guard to fulfill their requirement. We knew those people had a very slim possibility of going to Vietnam. It was true most took student deferments. I was fortunate that when it came my time, I had a very high number. I have to sympathize somewhat with what he was doing because I saw it all over the place. I accept the fact that he didn't serve.[51]

Four Bush stand patters: Carl Adams from group one, Penny Lobmon from group three, and Darlene Ross from group four, cited the draft story as another reason why they didn't trust Clinton to be commander in chief. Panelist Craig Koll, a member of group three, who was undecided before the general election, mentioned that Clinton's draft problems made him uncomfortable. At this point in the campaign, Koll began leaning toward George Bush.

Panelist Reaction To Perot's Return To The Race

On October 1, 1992 Ross Perot announced his return to the presidential campaign trail. There is some speculation that Perot merely took time off from the campaign in order to let the news media attacks blow over. In fact, the content analysis in Chapter 4 clearly shows that Perot generated very little news during the months of his hiatus. Furthermore, attack items involving Perot dropped close to zero in August and September.

Not all the panelists who initially supported Perot welcomed him back into the campaign, but five of the eighteen panelists expressed the notion that he would help press the two other major party candidates to be more upfront on the issues. As Carol Bach from the high political interest/difficult media access group commented, "I'm glad Perot has entered the race again it adds some fireworks. I'm glad he's still scaring both candidates. Someone has to mention the big D word, the deficit."[52] Likewise Marc Jackman from the same group said, "I was happy to see Perot back in the race. Perot is forcing the candidate and the media to focus on the economy and the debt. Both he and Clinton are right in this area."[53]

Craig Koll from the low interest/easy media access group speculated on why Perot rejoined the campaign, "I don't think he can win. I think it is good that he's back in. It's making the politicians try harder."[54] Likewise, Hilda Holmquist from the high political interest/difficult media access group stated:

> I think his coming back was calculated. Anybody who can spend six million dollars on a campaign like we spend six hundred dollars at Disney World is not any more in tune with this country than George Bush was. I think Ross Perot, for me, he really puts the screws to the candidates to fess up to what the issues are. I think he's a little crazy. He's been a one man show all his life so he'll do what he wants.[55]

Darlene Ross, a Bush supporter from the low political interest/ difficult media access group, was quite invalidating about the Perot re-entry. For Darlene the stories concerning Perot's unpresidential temperament clearly had an impact.: "I saw his temper tantrums. That's not the way a President should act. I don't know why he is running again."[56] Likewise, Carl Adams another Bush supporter from the high political interest/easy media access group succinctly said, "He's a joke still, in my opinion."[57] Ronald Burton a Perot supporter from the high political interest/easy media access group spoke metaphorically about Perot's October surprise:

> I used to work at an automobile rental agency. In that capacity, you need to make quick judgements in a matter of minutes as to who you can trust. I feel that the voting decision is similar. In Perot's case, why would you rent a car again to someone who didn't return a car the last time he was there?[58]

Deidre Utley another Bush supporter from the low political interest/difficult media access group was also negative on the Perot return: "I think it's a waste of money, time, and effort for him to get back in at the last minute. No man has ever gotten back in at the last minute and won a Presidency. I can't see wasting six million dollars on it."[59] Bill

Nystrum an early Perot backer from the low political interest/easy media access group echoed her comments: "It won't make any difference. He's wasting his time and his considerable wealth on what one might call a serendipitous adventure."[60]

Penny Lobmon also a Bush supporter and a fellow panelist in Nystrum's group scoffed at Perot's explanation that he left the race because of Bush's dirty tricks:.

> That was a really stupid move! For him to say it was based on his daughter's wedding and all kinds of dirty tricks, I think it hurt him a lot. It just shows his incompetence. I think he's just a little man with a lot to say. He'll never get anything done.[61]

Bettie Tisdale from the low political interest/difficult media access group incredulously asked, "Who is this Ross Perot? He should just leave President Bush alone and that, what's his name, Clinton, should let the man be, too."[62] Similarly, Sandra Sandelius said, "I will not support Perot. He is an independent and if he gets elected without having a party, I think it is not good for the country. I think that to support him would be to lose. It is necessary to have the whole support of an established party in order to get anything done."[63]

The most positive comments about Perot's re-entry back into the presidential campaign came from Maggie Gaylord, a member of the high political interest/difficult media access group:

> I think the man would be a wonderful, wonderful candidate if he could be dependable. I say dropping out and coming back in at this late date — I don't know what's going on in the man's mind. You know? I think that if he could take his business sense without being politically inclined and really make the difference, but I really, really don't know if the man is trustworthy or not.[64]

Presidential Debates Crowd Out October Attacks

In October the news sources contained a few residual stories about Clinton's draft status and character flaws as well as some renewed attacks about Perot's temperament and business practices. New attack items surfaced regarding Bush's involvement in both the Iran/Contra affair and the military build up in Iraq as well as Bush dirty tricks involving illegal searches through the passport files of both Clinton and Perot. All the media attention generated by Ross Perot's surprise re-entry back into the race, three Presidential debates, and one Vice Presidential debate seems to have suffocated panelist recollections of the Bush Iran contra and Iraqgate attack news items. (See Table 5.7)

The media consumption of the panelists during the presidential debates followed patterns observed during the two national conventions. As Table 5.6 demonstrates, in general, the high political interest groups watched all of the debates. The low political interest groups watched all or parts of the first Presidential debate, lost interest and did not watch the final debate forums.

Table 5.6: Panelist Exposure to the Presidential Debates

	Presidential Debate 1	V.P. Debate	Presidential Debate 2	Presidential Debate 3
Group 1				
Carl	X	X	X	X
Ron	X	X	X	
Bill	X	X	X	X
Pete	X	X	X	X
Leon	X	X	X	X
Group 2				
Carol	X	X	X	X
Marc	X	X		
Charles	X	X	X	X
Maggie				
Hilda	X	X	X	X
Group 3				
Penny	X	X		
Craig	X			
Elaine	X	X	X	
Bill	X			
Group 4				
Darlene	X	X		
Deidre	X			
Sandra	X		X	
Bettie	X			

Overall, of the three candidates in the presidential debates, Ross Perot made the most impact on the panelists, but the lackluster performance of Admiral James Stockdale in the Vice Presidential debate seemed to block panelists from taking the Perot campaign seriously. For example, Darlene Ross from the low interest/difficult access group said "that Stockdale man was just ridiculous."[65]

The addition of Ross Perot back into the race and the close scheduling of the debates, caused an information overload for the panelists. Carol Bach of the high interest/difficult access group seemed to sum up the frustrations of panelists who watched the debates:

> Three debates so close together was a little tedious. It was interesting to watch some of the group dynamics. Perot added some fireworks in the Presidential debates. His choice of running mate is unfortunate. I was very uncomfortable during the Vice Presidential debates, especially watching Quayle who seems to have studied Reagan tapes. It was eerie. But the debates did not influence my decision at all. [66]

However, Ross Perot's debate performance favorably impacted Craig Koll of the low interest/easy access group.and Marc Jackman from the high interest/difficult access group. Jackman was impressed with both Perot and Clinton and displeased by Bush:

> Perot seemed more in touch with ordinary people. He made sense to me on issues such as the economy and the debt. I believe Bush spent too much time on the character issue and not enough time on the real issues. Even though I hear that the economy has improved, Clinton kept reminding me that it should be better. You know, too many Americans are out of work or under-employed.[67]

Deidre Utley, another member of the low interest/difficult access group, only saw part of the first debate. At this point in the campaign, Utley became discouraged about Bush's re-election prospects and blamed Perot: "I watched the first hour and gave up. I'm mad at Perot. Perot is the reason Bush is going to lose the election."[68] Sandra Sandelius, another member of the low interest/difficult access group went a step further and predicted the ultimate victor in the election, "I have the feeling that Clinton will win. One reason is that he is more secure and the other is that he has more presence than the other presidential candidates."[69]

Panelist Reaction To The Last Minute Ad Blitz

Often voters have difficulty differentiating between political spots and television campaign news. As Jamieson comments: "Like pack rats, voters gather bits and pieces of political information and store them in a single place. Lost in the storage is a clear recall of where this or that 'fact' came. Information obtained from news mixes with that from ads, for example."[70]

Ironically, the panelists in this study reacted most vigorously to a paid political spot that was unique to South Carolina and unrelated to the presidential contest. These opinions are relevant to my research, because they give us further insight into how the panelists in this study process attack information.

Even though interview questions to the panelists were limited to information concerning the Presidential election, seven of the eighteen panelists expressed unsolicited opinions on a campaign advertisement produced for Tommy Hartnett, a Republican United States Senate candidate in South Carolina. The spot charged that the incumbent, Senator Ernest Hollings, supported a gay rights quota bill. The controversial Hartnett ad generated several news stories on local television newscasts and in the Columbia newspapers.

An interesting pattern emerged among the panelists who saw the spot. Each of the African American panelists: Bill Creighton of group one, Pete Diedrich of group one, Maggie Gaylord of group two, Bettie Tisdale of group four, and three white female panelists: Carol Bach of group two, Hilda Holmquist of group two, and Elaine Miller of group three derided the Hartnett ad. At least two of these panelists claimed the ad affected their vote choice. Maggie Gaylord and Hilda Holmquist said they were going to vote for Hartnett until that spot ran. As Maggie stated, "If he discriminates against gays, he'll discriminate against anyone."[71]

At the presidential campaign level, only one panelist cited a specific political advertisement as directly affecting her vote choice. Bettie Tisdale, a member of the low interest/difficult access group and a disabled mother dependent upon social services, decided to vote against Clinton early in the campaign. Bettie was troubled by the Clinton advertisements during the primary season which promised a get tough approach regarding welfare. She said, "I saw those ads. He doesn't get it. I want to work. I think people should work, but I have a disability and can't work. What am I gonna do?"[72]

Five panelists stated that they enjoyed Ross Perot's special half hour "infomercials." Two of the five, Carl Adams and Ron Burton, were from the high interest/easy access group. One, Marc Jackman, was from the high interest/difficult access group. Another, Penny Lobmon, was from the low interest/easy access group. The fifth, Darlene Ross, was from the low interest/difficult access group.

News items questioning Clinton's trustability and attack ads such as "Why Voters Don't Trust Bill Clinton" produced for the Bush campaign only seemed to reinforce the Bush "stand-patters," voters who were predisposed toward Bush as indicated in their initial questionnaires. Penny Lobmon of the low interest/easy access group frequently repeated that she did not trust Clinton. That statement seemed to be a mantra for the Bush stand-patters.

Attack Items And Panelist Vote Choice

Table 5.7: Attack Topics Mentioned By Panelists

Key: 1. Bush POW-MIA remarks 2. Bush campaign staff dissention 3. Bush campaign dirty tricks 4. Bush alleged adultery 5. Bush and Iran/Contra 6. Bush and Iraqgate 7. Clinton's extra marital affairs 8. Clinton's Vietnam Draft Status 9. Clinton's character flaws 10. Clinton's overseas student demonstrations 11. Perot's NAACP Speech 12. Perot's investigations and questionable business practices 13. Perot's unpresidential temperament 14. Perot campaign staff dissention

	1	2	3	4	5	6	7	8	9	10	11	12	13	14
G1														
CA		X	X	X	X	X	X	X	X			X	X	X
RB		X	X	X	X			X	X				X	X
BC		X	X	X				X	X	X		X	X	X	X
PD		X	X	X	X			X	X	X		X	X	X	X
LE		X	X	X					X	X	X		X	X	X
G2														
CB		X	X	X	X			X	X				X	X	X
MJ	X	X	X	X				X	X	X			X	X	X
CI		X	X	X		X	X	X	X				X	X	X
MG		X	X	X				X	X	X	X			X	X
HH		X	X	X	X			X	X	X			X	X	X

Key: 1. Bush POW-MIA remarks 2. Bush campaign staff dissention 3. Bush campaign dirty tricks 4. Bush alleged adultery 5. Bush and Iran/Contra 6. Bush and Iraqgate 7. Clinton's extra marital affairs 8. Clinton's Vietnam Draft Status 9. Clinton's character flaws 10. Clinton's overseas student demonstrations 11. Perot's NAACP Speech 12. Perot's investigations and questionable business practices 13. Perot's unpresidential temperament 14. Perot campaign staff dissention

	1	2	3	4	5	6	7	8	9	10	11	12	13	14
G3														
PL	X	X	X				X	X				X	X	X
CK	X	X	X				X	X	X			X	X	X
EM	X	X	X	X			X	X	X		X	X	X	X
BN	X		X				X	X				X	X	X
G4														
DR	X		X				X	X	X				X	X
DU	X		X				X	X	X				X	X
SS	X		X	X			X	X	X			X	X	X
BT		X	X				X		X				X	

As Table 5.7 shows, attack items involving verbal miscues such as Bush's remark to POW-MIA families and Perot's speech to the NAACP were only mentioned by a few of the panelists. Both these events were relatively short-lived and the panelists may not have deemed them as important campaign developments. Moreover, few panelists recalled attack stories about Bush and the Iran/Contra affair(#5), the Iraqgate scandal (#6), and Clinton's involvement in overseas demonstrations as a college student (#10).

There are two plausible explanations as to why these last three topics did not reach the panelists uniformly. First, as mentioned earlier in this report, these items emerged emerged late in the campaign when panelists were deluged with campaign news information. Second, a more subtle analysis suggests that these three attack items involved dated information and more complex issue-oriented attack topics. For example, the Iran/Contra matter had already been widely scrutinized in the 1988 presidential election. The evidence linking Bush to the military build up in Iraq was somewhat clouded. Moreover, after the success of Desert Storm, this information may not have seemed credible to the panelists. Likewise, news reports about Bill Clinton's student participation in overseas demonstrations many years ago might also have been viewed by the panelists as trivial matters at such a late stage in the campaign.

However, attack news reports of staff turmoil in the Bush campaign (#2) and Perot organization (#14) clearly resonated with the panelists. These items are more closely associated with the horserace aspect of the campaign which may explain why more panelists mentioned them during the interviews. Likewise, the major character attack news items (#4) Bush's alleged adultery, (#8) Clinton's Vietnam draft problems, (#9) Clinton's character flaws, and (#13) Perot's unpresidential temperament caught nearly universal attention of the panelists in this study. The increased attention to the character attack topics might be explained by a common cognitive strategy utilized by the panelists. As Table 5.8 reveals, 16 of the 18 panelists routinely employed personal evaluations of the candidates; therefore, there seems to be a link between person schemas and attention to attack journalism focusing on candidate character questions.

Table 5.8: Attack exposure, information processing schemas, & vote choice

	Panelist Initial Choice	Total Attack Topics	#Attacks Against Choice	Utilized Person Schemas	Utilized Issue Schemas	Utilized Party Schemas	Panelist Final Vote
G 1							
Carl	Bush	11	5	X	X	X	Bush
Ron	Perot	09	2	X	X		Clinton
Bill	Perot	10	4	X	X	X	Clinton
Pete	Clinton	11	3	X	X		Clinton
Leon	?	09	n/a	X	X		Clinton
G 2							
Carol	Perot	09	3		X	X	Clinton
Marc	Perot	10	3	X	X		Perot
Charles	Perot	10	3	X	X	X	Clinton
Maggie	?	08	n/a	X	X		write-in
Hilda	?	10	n/a	X	X		Clinton
G 3							
Penny	Bush	08	3	X		X	Bush
Craig	?	09	n/a	X	X	X	Bush
Elaine	Clinton	11	3	X	X		Clinton
Bill	Perot	07	3		X	X	no vote

	Panelist Initial Choice	Total Attack Topics	#Attacks Against Choice	Utilized Person Schemas	Utilized Issue Schemas	Utilized Party Schemas	Panelist Final Vote
G 4							
Darlene	Bush	07	2	X	X	X	Bush
Deidre	Bush	07	2	X		X	Bush
Sandra	?	09	3	X	X	X	Bush
Bettie	Bush	05	2	X	X		Bush

*Note: As in Table 5.7, there were 14 total attack topics.

High political interest/Easy media access group vote

As Tables 5.7 and 5.8 show, the members of group one mentioned most of the attack topics that emerged during the 1992 general election. These panelists relied mainly on person schemas and issue schemas in order to process campaign news information. Panelist Carl Adams had expressed concerns throughout the campaign about the characters of both Clinton and Perot. Adams stood pat and voted to re-elect President Bush. He claimed to recognize the President's flaws, but felt most of Bush's political problems were due to the Democrats in Congress.

Ronald Burton and Bill Creighton switched from Ross Perot to Bill Clinton. Burton and Creighton were drawn to Perot as a change agent, but lost enthusiasm for his candidacy when he dropped out. They switched to Clinton, because of his economic issue stances. Pete Diedrich stood pat throughout the election and voted for Clinton. Leon Evans moved from undecided and cast his vote for Clinton/Gore. Evans wanted to give the new generation a chance to solve the nation's complex problems.

High political interest/Difficult media access group vote

As Tables 5.7 and 5.8 demonstrate, the members of group two also recalled the vast majority of the 1992 attack topics. These panelists also relied primarily on person schemas and issue schemas as strategies to process the 1992 election news information. Two panelists in group two switched from Ross Perot to Bill Clinton. Perot's outsider status appealed to these two panelists early in the campaign. However, after Perot dropped out, Bach and Ippolitos were convinced that Clinton was the only candidate with the credibility to repair the American economy.

Marc Jackman stuck with Perot, but he was unsure about his vote until the very last minute: "I voted for Perot because he is practical, not a regular politician, and I think only he can break up the special interest problem in Washington. I did not expect him to win and I consider my vote a protest vote against the Washington establishment. Both Clinton and Bush are part of that establishment in my opinion."[73] Maggie Gaylord who was undecided throughout the election, cast a write-in protest vote, because she was still fed up with the politics at the end of the campaign. She wanted to vote for Perot, but in her view, he was just too unreliable. Hilda Holmquist, moved from undecided at the start of the campaign and voted for Clinton at the polls. Holmquist was consistently negative toward Bush. Early on, she was interested in Perot, but lost interest due to his lack of issue specifics.

Low political interest/Easy media access group vote

Table 5.8 shows that there was a slight drop in the total number of attack topics mentioned by the panelists in group three. Moreover, the panelists employed a more even mix of person, issue, and political party schemas in order to process the election news information. Panelist Penny Lobmon stood pat and voted to re-elect George Bush. Lobmon frequently mentioned that she did not trust Clinton. Likewise, throughout the course of the 1992 election, she was quite critical of Perot due to reports about his unpresidential temperament.

Craig Koll moved from undecided and voted for President Bush. Koll was very interested in the Perot campaign until he dropped out of the race. Like Lobmon, Koll distrusted Clinton and eventually settled on Bush. Elaine Miller stood pat with Bill Clinton, because of Clinton's issue stances. She expressed a strong personal distaste for George Bush and questioned Perot's ties to big business. Finally, Bill Nystrum, who had originally expressed support for Perot, did not vote in the 1992 general election. He remained the most cynical about the political process throughout the election.

Low political interest/Difficult media access group vote

Table 5.8 shows that the panelists in group four had the lowest attack topic totals. However, these panelists mentioned most of the attack topics involving character items. Three of the four members of this group also routinely utilized political party schemas when processing 1992 campaign news information. This group had the largest share of stand-patters. Three of the four panelists: Darlene Ross, Deidre Utley, and Bettie Tisdale stood pat to re-elect Bush. Each was openly critical of both Clinton and Perot during the campaign, although Tisdale remained relatively uninformed about the Perot candidacy throughout the election. Sandra Sandelius who was undecided in her initial questionnaire eventually cast her vote for George Bush. Sandelius respected Bush as a world leader, but expressed disappointment that he was not more specific about his platform during the campaign.

Summary of panelist vote choice

As Table 5.8 indicates, the attack news exposure did not affect final vote choice evenly across the board. Perot experienced the greatest shift in support over the course of the campaign. Five out of the six panelists who expressed support for his candidacy in their initial questionnaires did not vote for him after he withdrew from the race in July during the Democratic National Convention. Four switched to Bill Clinton. Overall, the panelists who abandoned Perot tended to accentuate candidate personality and issue positions. These panelists relied less on political parties for voting cues.

A total of eight panelists voted for the Arkansas Governor Bill Clinton, even though they were aware of a majority of the attack items about him. With these panelists, the shield for Clinton against the attacks seemed to be economic issues. The panelists who voted for Clinton were able to prioritize the election news information about him. With these panelists, the status of the American economy and Clinton's pledges to repair it were more important than questions about his character.

Furthermore, It is also interesting to note that of the seven panelists who voted for George Bush, only Bettie Tisdale, did not employ a party information processing schema. The panelists in this study who relied heavily on political party schemas as a means to process campaign news information were able to dismiss the attack information about George Bush. This suggests that strong Republican party affiliation may circumvent voter information processing of attack journalism against Republican candidates.

Now having examined the results of the media content analysis in Chapter 4 and the analysis of the panelist interviews in Chapter 5, the final chapter will discuss the implications of these findings and discuss possible improvements for the Presidential selection process in the United States.

Notes:

[1] Interview on July 22, 1992.
[2] Interview on July 23, 1992.
[3] Interview on July 19, 1992.
[4] Interview on July 20, 1992.
[5] Interview on July 22, 1992.
[6] Interview on July 19, 1992.
[7] Interview on July 19, 1992.
[8] Interview on July 19, 1992.
[9] Interview on July 23, 1992.
[10] Interview on July 20, 1992.
[11] Interview on July 19, 1992.
[12] Interview on July 20, 1992.
[13] Interview on July 21, 1992.
[14] Interview on July 20, 1992.
[15] Interview on July 19, 1992.
[16] Interview on July 21, 1992.
[17] Interview on July 19, 1992.
[18] Interview on July 23, 1992.
[19] Interview on July 21, 1992.
[20] Interview on July 21, 1992.
[21] Interview on July 19, 1992.
[22] Interview on July 22, 1992.
[23] Interview on July 22, 1992.
[24] Interview on July 20, 1992.
[25] Interview on July 20, 1992.
[26] Interview on July 19, 1992.
[27] Interview on July 23, 1992.
[28] Interview on July 21, 1992.
[29] Interview on July 20, 1992.
[30] Interview on July 20, 1992.
[31] Interview on July 21, 1992.
[32] Interview on July 22, 1992.
[33] Interview on July 20, 1992.
[34] Interview on July 20, 1992.
[35] Interview on August 14, 1992.
[36] Interview on August 19, 1992.
[37] Interview on August 15, 1992.
[38] Interview on August 13, 1992.

[39]Interview on August 21, 1992.
[40]Interview on August 13, 1992.
[41]Interview on August 21, 1992.
[42]Interview on August 22, 1992.
[43]Interview on August 20, 1992.
[44]Interview on August 21, 1992.
[45]Interview on August 31, 1992.
[46]Interview on August 30, 1992.
[47]Interview on August 23, 1992.
[48]Interview on August 19, 1992.
[49]Interview on October 24, 1992.
[50]Interview on September 1, 1992.
[51]Interview on September 16, 1992.
[52]Interview on October 2, 1992.
[53]Interview on October 5, 1992.
[54]Interview on October 13, 1992.
[55]Interview on October 15, 1992.
[56]Interview on October 3, 1992.
[57]Interview on October 9, 1992.
[58]Interview on October 2, 1992.
[59]Interview on October 5, 1992.
[60]Interview on October 13, 1992.
[61]Interview on October 12, 1992.
[62]Interview on October 2, 1992.
[63]Interview on October 11, 1992.
[64]Interview on October 9, 1992.
[65]Interview on October 23, 1992.
[66]Interview on October 24, 1992.
[67]Interview on October 23, 1992.
[68]Interview on October 22, 1992.
[69]Interview on October 25, 1992.
[70]Jamieson, Kathleen Hall, *Dirty Politics: Deception, Distraction, and Democracy,* 1st edition, Oxford University Press, 1992:17.
[71]Interview on October 25, 1992.
[72]Interview on July 20, 1992.
[73]Interview on November 7, 1992.

Chapter 6

Conclusion

The 1992 Presidential contest provided several episodes of attack journalism. The most widely recognized instances being items such as draft-dodging, drug use, and alleged adultery on the part of both Bill Clinton and President Bush, and questions involving Ross Perot's temperament. However, the eighteen panelists in this study somehow waded through the "sleaze" in search of more appropriate election news information. As panelist Leon Evans explained, the attack news items based on character flaws were "distractions" from the important issues facing the nation.

The findings in this study concerning the cognitive information processing of the panelists are compatible with "The Manhattan Project," an intensive internal research project on voter attitudes about Bill Clinton conducted by consultants working for the Clinton campaign during the general election.[1] These findings are also in agreement with polling throughout the campaign. For example, a Time/CNN poll taken before the New Hampshire primary found that 82% of the respondents stated that the media paid too much attention to the personal lives of the candidates.[2]

However, even with some similarities in the media coverage regarding personal scandals, there were fundamental differences between the 1992 contest and the widely criticized 1988 campaign. First, as cited in Chapter Two of this report, members of the press became painfully aware of their shortcomings in 1988 and did attempt to provide better campaign coverage in 1992. For example, researchers at The Freedom Forum Media Studies Center interviewed over twenty news elites who cited at least seven lessons they had learned from 1988 campaign coverage: 1. The press focused too much attention on the horserace aspect of the campaign; 2. The press many times allowed itself to be utilized as a vehicle for meaningless photo opportunities; 3. The news media did not cover candidate positions on the issues enough; 4. The press failed to adequately analyze campaign advertising and refute false claims; 5. The news media seemed to leave the concerns of the voters out of the picture spending too much time on polls and pundits; 6. The press paid too much attention to scandalous details of candidate's background; and 7. Candidate soundbites shrank even smaller to an average of nine seconds.[3]

Beyond the press coverage, perhaps the most important differences between the 1992 election and the 1988 campaign were the levels of economic stress that confronted the voters and the unique third party addition of Ross Perot. The findings of this dissertation study seem to confirm two studies by Gregory B. Markus claiming that campaigns tend to heighten voter awareness of economic issues and that individuals link the performance of the incumbent to the status of the economy.[4] Throughout the interview process, all eighteen panelists made continued reference to the sour economy during the 1992 campaign. Moreover, the fact that Bill Clinton survived charges like draft-dodging and womanizing that had vaporized past presidential candidacies, may bode well for future campaigns and help to bolster the argument that voters are indeed fairly sophisticated information processors who can look past the tabloid news and evaluate candidacies in a more creditable fashion.

Although many panelists indicated in their initial questionnaire that they listened to radio reports about the campaign, not one panelist mentioned radio as the source of information for any of the events we discussed during our interviews. This is compatible with a poll constructed by Times Mirror during the primaries which found that 83% of the respondents cited television as the source of information for the presidential campaign, 48% chose newspapers, 14% selected radio, and 4% cited magazines. Of the 83% who mentioned television as the major source of presidential campaign information, 49% said network news was the main source of information, 39% cited local news and 36% selected CNN.[5] Similarly, my research seems consistent with a study conducted by Strate, Ford, and Jankowski indicating that there is a gender gap between men and women concerning consumption of print media to follow public affairs.[6] This may help explain why groupings in this study, based on the initial questionnaire, resulted in all male panelists in the high-interest/easy access group and all female panelists in the low-interest/difficult access group. Furthermore, among all the panelists in this study, television news or television programs were cited most frequently as the source of election information with occasional references to newspaper or magazine articles. Newspapers were used as research tools in order to flesh out information gleaned from television reports. For example, panelists: Ronald Burton, Leon Evans, Charles Ippolitos, and Sandra Sandelius commented throughout the campaign that they planned to study accumulated newspaper reports before making a final voting decision. The media consumption pattern of the panelists concerning television, newspapers, and radio broadcasts also seems to echo the results of a 1990 study by Drew and Weaver who found that newspapers are more likely to influence cognitive learning, television influences both cognitive learning and attitudes, and radio is less influential.[7]

The interview findings in Chapter 5 support my hypothesis that certain attack stories catalyze the attention of voters regardless of political interest and media access. Only one panelist, Bettie Tisdale, was not fully aware of Ross Perot's rocky withdrawal from and surprise re-entry back into the contest. Again, only one panelist, Bill Nystrum, did not mention the allegations of adultery that engulfed the Bush campaign in mid August. All panelists mentioned, at some point during the interview process, similar charges concerning marital infidelity on the part of Bill Clinton that arose initially during the Democratic primaries. Similarly, all panelists talked of the controversy concerning Clinton's Vietnam draft status which also emerged during the New Hampshire primary and continued throughout the general election.

However, while attack stories involving character items generally caught the attention of the panelists regardless of political interest or media access, these items did not seem to affect final vote choice evenly across the board as I predicted. The feeding frenzies (accompanied by his own mercurial behavior) did severely damage the support for Ross Perot among those panelists who indicated support for him on their initial questionnaires, but potentially scandalous incidents involving both Clinton and Bush only seemed to resonate with panel members who were already predisposed against the candidate in question during the media feeding frenzies. The voters themselves may have learned from previous campaigns to disregard sensational tabloid information about the candidates. Similarly, the press in 1992 deserves partial credit for pre-empting and limiting paid personal attacks by the candidates by means of monitoring paid political advertisements and broadcasting veracity checks with critiques of new political commercials.

Again, thanks to Ross Perot, the candidates themselves learned to bypass the attack pack of reporters by utilizing non-traditional media outlets such as *Larry King Live,* MTV, and morning talk shows in an effort to speak directly with the American people. Researchers at The Freedom Forum Media Studies Center claim that these talk shows are the new "whistle-stops on the campaign trail."[8] However, their research also noted a significant reluctance on the part of President Bush to appear on the non-traditional talk show forums.[9] As the Freedom Forum Research Group reports, such formats have several advantages: free airtime for candidates, uninterrupted dialogue, viewer participation, and raw presentation of the candidates without a journalistic filter. Moreover, the media political directors at ABC, CBS, and NBC stated that the rise of television talk shows was a positive development and not a threat to their news efforts.[10] Neuman contends that future campaigns may actually benefit from these non-traditional media outlets and new media technologies. The mass audience may eventually have dozens of television information sources from which to choose. Neuman also cites the promise of interactive devices as keys to increased educational opportunities for television viewers.[11] More information sources and a better educated audience might lead to more issue oriented presidential campaigns.

However, Neuman also explains possible negative social effects of new media technology. The mass media may shift to waves of specialized narrow-interest channels resulting in an information overload that renders the audience "helpless."[12] But the information overload may not be experienced by everyone. Some individuals may get even less information since the rise of new technologies may result in the formation of a new "information underclass" consisting of citizens who can not afford the computer hardware and training in order to gain the skills to operate it.[13] Political processes and institutions may be radically altered by the new media. For example, political parties may completely whither away as the media might become the only intercessory between candidates and voters. The executive branch may become even more powerful because of the easy media focus on the President. American political culture may shift to democracy without deliberation as interactive television could create unreasonable expectations for instant results.[14]

Regardless of what the future holds, the present changes in media coverage effect both political campaigns and the governing process. Dallek, a presidential historian at the University of California at Los Angeles, comments on the impact of attack journalism on both campaigning and governing:

> After the searing events of the last 30 years, with many revelations of secret government, dirty tricks and cover ups, the presidency is now damaged goods and the occupants of the office a certain target when any hint of personal impropriety, past or present, surfaces. Clinton, and all future candidates for, and occupants of, the office need to steel themselves for this unpleasant truth. Since we are not likely to see many saints running for the presidency in the foreseeable future, the candidate who do run would do well to develop the thickest possible skins against the charges inevitably hurled at them. More important, the public and the media should understand that president bashing may satisfy some current exaggerated passion for righteous public servants. But it will prove to be an imperfect way to conduct the country's urgent business. No one wants to call a moratorium on publicizing and, if need be, prosecuting wrongdoing by politicians. But greater common sense in scrutinizing personal misdeeds by potential and sitting presidents can save the incumbents and the country from considerable grief.[15]

Correcting The Disequilibrium

Patterson suggests that the decline of the political parties and the increasing influence of the mass media undermine the American way of electing a chief executive. But he says the solution lies in reform of the election process not in changes in the news media:

> After every presidential election scholars and pundits, along with many journalists, say that campaigns would be better if only the press would report them differently. The assumption underlying this conclusion is that the press has the ability to organize the choices

facing the voters. The burden on the media is particularly severe during the nominating phase. Within the limited time it has to communicate with the voters, the press is expected to create an electorate that can understand what a half-dozen previously unfamiliar candidates represent and can calculate the possible outcomes of a multi-candidate race.[16]

Patterson states that the press can and should improve presidential campaign coverage, but elections will continue in disarray until improvements are made to diminish the media's role as political intermediary. He explains that the easiest way to accomplish this goal is to shorten the nomination process by conducting regional primaries or one nation primary.[17] Likewise Cronin and Loevy discuss the possibility of creating a three stage presidential process by adding a pre-primary convention and replacing the six month series of individual primaries with a national primary lasting six to eight weeks. They suggest that this will reduce media influence and return to a nominating rather than a ratifying convention.[18]

A less radical way to modify the primary process and still maintain Cronin and Loevy's three tiered suggestion would be to convene a caucus of party elites (ex officio or "super delegates") before the primary season and require presidential aspirants to achieve a threshold of support in order to merit access to state ballots under either of the major party labels. The proposal is to return partially to the "King Caucus" system that briefly held in the American politics before political conventions became the primary mechanism for the nomination process. This idea would strengthen political parties by allowing party elites more opportunity to screen the candidates before the primary season. The current string of primaries and caucuses as well as the convention process could remain in the same.

The theory underlying the new King Caucus would be to replace the media's vetting of candidates that now unfolds unsystematically during the individual primaries with a more formal screening process by party officials. The party caucus would help American political parties to regain some control over the nomination process. The assumption being that candidates with embarrassing scandals would have difficulty achieving a minimum threshold of support among the party elites. However, the threshold could be kept to a minimum of 5 to 15% of the super delegates so that the maximum number of contenders would be available. Candidates failing to achieve the threshold would be denied access to primary ballots under that party's banner.

Likewise, changes outside the electoral process might be implemented in order to balance the campaign system. Sabato argues that the reconfiguration of the media industry and a loosening of libel laws beginning in 1964 created campaign news coverage that is entertainment oriented and sensationalist. [19]With the proliferation of talk shows, the onset of "checkbook" journalism in which news sources are paid large sums of money for information, the intense competition resulting in a lightning speed of information flow, it may be time now to tighten libel laws and allow political candidates greater opportunity to seek legal redress when false and misleading news items about their personal lives are reported. Such changes may provide an economic incentive for media outlets to be more diligent and responsible in political campaign coverage. However, any change extending personal privacy rights for candidates must ensure that the press can vigorously scrutinize illegal or unethical conduct on the part of public officials. Sabato suggests eight criterion in which a candidate's private life might be subject to publication and broadcast, five areas in which a candidate's private life should be shielded from publication or broadcast, and four additional provisions and qualifiers in the "remedies" chapter of *Feeding Frenzy*.[20] These guidelines might provide the basis for future changes in libel law that may indeed act as a remedy for attack journalism.

Overall, there is reason to be optimistic about the future of American presidential elections. As seen in this study, voters are able to process political news rather competently. The eighteen panelists in this study were able to disregard most of the tabloid information in their final vote choice. The consensus among media scholars is that the press should continue efforts to improve campaign coverage, but significant improvements will require structural changes in the electoral process. The new media holds both promise for and danger to our democratic processes and institutions. It is my strong belief that continued scholarly research in this area can help to improve presidential campaign coverage in the future and safeguard the integrity of the democratic voting process.

Notes:

[1]Germond, Jack W. and Jules Witcover, *Mad As Hell: Revolt at the Ballot Box 1992,* Warner Books, 1993:282.

[2]FitzSimon, Martha, "Covering the Presidential Primaries, *The Media and Campaign '92: A Series of Special Election Reports,* The Freedom Forum Media Studies Center, Columbia University , June 1992:53

[3]Ibid:28

[4]See Markus, Gregory B. "Political Attitudes During an Election Year: A Report on the 1980 NES Panel Study," *American Political Science Review, 76,* 1982:538-60; "The Impact of Personal and Economic Conditions on the Presidential Vote: A Pooled Cross Sectional Analysis," *American Journal of Political Science, 32,* 1988:137-154.

[5]See FitzSimon, Martha, "Covering the Presidential Primaries," *The Media and Campaign '92: A Series of Special Election Reports,* The Freedom Forum Media Studies Center, Columbia University, June 1992:57.

[6]Strate, John M., Coit Cook Ford III, and Thomas B. Jankowski, "Women's Use of Print Media to Follow Politics," *Social Science Quarterly,* 75:1, March 1994: 166-186.

[7]Drew, Dan and David Weaver, "Media Attention, Media Exposure, and Media Effects," *Journalism Quarterly,* 67:4, 1990:740-748

[8]FitzSimon, Martha, "An Uncertain Season-Reporting in the Postprimary Period,"*The Media and Campaign '92,* The Freedom Forum Media Studies Center, September 1992:8.

[9]Ibid:24.

[10]Ibid:25-27.

[11]Neuman, W. Russell, *The Future of the Mass Audience,* Cambridge University Press, 1991:106.

[12]Ibid:81

[13]Ibid:5

[14]Ibid:6

[15]Dallek, Robert "The Presidency: Mean to Me," *The Boston Sunday Globe,* May 15, 1994: 73,76.

[16]Patterson, Thomas E. *Out of Order: How the decline of the political parties and the growing power of the news media undermine the American way of electing presidents,* Alfred A. Knopf, Inc., 1993:26.

[17]Ibid:209

[18]DiClerico, Robert E. *Analyzing The Presidency,* The Dushkin Publishing Group, 1990:28

[19]McCubbins, Matthew D. *Under The Watchful Eye: Managing Presidential Campaigns in the Television Era,* CQ Press, 1992:127.

[20]Sabato, Larry J. *Feeding Frenzy: How Attack Journalism Has Transformed American Politics,* The Free Press, 1991:218-219.

Appendix A

QUESTIONNAIRE

1. Some people seem to follow what's going on in government and public affairs whether there's an election going on or not. Others aren't that interested. Would you say that you follow government and public affairs:

   a. most of the time   b. some of the time
   c. only now and then   d. hardly at all

2. Some people don't pay much attention to campaigns. How about you? In the campaign this year, would you say you are:

   a.   very much interested   b. somewhat interested
   c.   not much interested

3. How much would you say that you personally care how the presidential election comes out?

   a. very much   b. not very much

4. How often do you discuss politics with your family or friends?

   a. everyday   b. 3 or 4 times a week
   c. once or twice a week   d. less than once a week

5. This question concerns various public figures. We want to see how much information about them gets out to the public from television, newspapers, and the like. Write the job or position each person holds next to their name. If you don't know just leave it blank.

a. Tom Foley   b. John Major
b. Yasser Arafat   c. Alan Greenspan

6. Do you happen to know which party has the most members in the House of Representatives in Washington?

   a. Republicans   b. Democrats

7. Do you happen to know which party has the most members in the U. S. Senate?

   a. Republicans   b. Democrats

8. In 1988, George Bush ran on the Republican ticket against Michael Dukakis for the Democrats. Which candidate did you vote for?

   a. Bush   b. Dukakis
   c. did not vote   d. can't remember for sure

9. If the 1992 presidential election were held today, who would you vote for?

   a. Bush (R)   b. Clinton (D)
   c. Perot (I)   d. Undecided

10. How many days in the past week did you watch national news on TV?

    a. everyday   b. 3 or 4 times
    c. once   d. none

11. How much attention did you pay to news on TV about the campaign for President?

    a. very much   b. some   c. not much

12. Did you watch any programs about the campaign on television? Would you say you watched:

a. a good many   b. several
c. just one or two   d. none

13. How many days in the past week did you read a daily newspaper?

_____

14. Which newspaper or papers did you read? _____

_____

15. How much attention did you pay to newspaper articles about the campaign for President?

    a. a great deal   b. several
    c. just one or two   d. none

16. Did you listen to any speeches or discussions about the campaign on radio? Would you say you listened to:

    a. a good many   b. several
    c. just one or two   d. none

17. How about magazines — did you read about the campaign in any magazines? How much attention did you pay to articles about the campaign for President?

    a. a great deal   b. some
    c. very little   d. none

PERSONAL DATA

(This information is for statistical purposes only and will be kept strictly confidential)

18. Age: a. 18-25   b. 26-35 c. 36-45 d. 46-60 e. 60+

19. Education: What is the highest grade of school or year of college you have completed? _____

20. We'd like to know if you are:

a. in school   b. working   c. temporarily laid off d. unemployed
e. retired   f. permanently disabled   g. at home with children

21. What is your occupation?_____

22. Race: a. American Indian or Alaskan native b. Hispanic
    c. African American d. Caucasian e. Asian or Pacific Islander
    f. Other

23. Sex: a. male   b. female

24. Would you be willing to participate in a more in-depth study of
    this year's presidential election consisting of a personal interview
    every two weeks from late July until the general election in early
    November?

    a. yes   b. no thank you

25. If you wish to participate further in this study, please complete the
    consent section below:

Signature _____ Date_____

Printed Name _____

Address _____

Phone (h)_____ (w)_____

Best time and day to call _____

THANK YOU!

Please return questionnaire in the self-addressed envelope enclosed.

Appendix B

INTERVIEW QUESTIONS

1. Reminder of confidentiality and permission to record.
2. If some of your friends were away, and wanted to know what was going on in the presidential campaign, what would you tell them?
3. How would you describe Bush, Clinton, and Perot to your friends?
4. What does "political party" mean to you?
5. Generally speaking, do you usually consider yourself as a Democrat, Republican, Independent, or something else?
6. What do you think are the most important problems facing the country? Of those you mentioned, what would you consider to be the single most important problem?
7. How good a job is the government doing to solve the problems you mentioned?
8. Which political party do you think would be likely to get the government moving to deal with these problems? Which candidate would be more likely to get the government moving to deal with these problems?
9. Do you think most of the people running the government are crooked, only a few, or hardly any of them are crooked?
10. What specific newspaper(s), local TV news, national news, radio stations, and news magazines do you follow regularly?
11. If an important event were happening, where would you seek information?
12. Why do you trust this source the most?
13. Were there any important events or issues that you noticed this week? Where did you hear about this?
14. Did any of the presidential candidates address issues this week that are important to you? Were there events or issues that were ignored by the candidates or the press?

15. Did you follow the Democratic/Republican convention? Which station did you watch it on?
16. Did you watch the debates? Which station did you watch them on? What was your reaction?
17. Did you see any political advertisements this week? Can you describe it for me? What do you think of that ad?
18. Are you satisfied with the media coverage of the campaign? Are you getting the information you need to make a decision?
19. (If panelist mentioned a specific controversy) Are you satisfied with the candidate's explanation of this event? Do you think this is an appropriate story for the media to report?
20. Have you made a decision on which candidate you will support? Why have you selected this candidate?
21. Did you vote? Who did you vote for and why did you vote for him?

Bibliography

Abramson, Jeffery B., Christopher Arterton, and Gary R. Orren, *The Electronic Commonwealth,* Basic Books, 1st edition, 1988.

"Air Wars Turn Nasty with Misleading Attacks," *The State,* October 17, 1992:10A.

Aldrich, John H., *Before the Convention: Strategies and Choices in Presidential Nomination Campaigns,* 5th edition, The University of Chicago Press, 1980.

Aldrich, John H. *Before the Convention,* University of Chicago Press, 5th edition, 1987.

Alger, Dean E. *The Media and Politics,* Prentice-Hall, 1st edition, 1989.

Arterton, F. Christopher, "Campaign '92: Strategies and Tactics," In *The Election of 1992,* 1st edition, Chatham House, 1993: 74-109.

Baer, Susan, "Slick Willie Transformed into a Strapping Contender," *The State,* August 2, 1992: 12A.

Bagdikian, Ben H. *The Media Monopoly,* Beacon Press, 1st edition, 1990.

Bailey, Doug, "The Third Wheel That May Help This Shebang Run Better," *Washington Post National Weekly,* June 15-21,1992:24.

Balz, Dan and Richard Morin, "An Electorate Ready to Revolt," *Washington Post National Weekly,* November 11-17,1991:6.

Balz, Dan and Thomas B. Edsall, "Heading South Where Things Heat Up," *Washington Post National Weekly,* February 24-March 1,1992:7.

Balz, Dan, "The Party is Betting Youth is the Ticket," *Washington Post National Weekly,* July 13-19,1992:8.

Balz, Dan, "In Media Res: If You Can't Beat 'Em, Bypass 'Em," *Washington Post National Weekly,* May 25-31,1992:12.

Barber, James David, *The Pulse of Politics: Electing Presidents in the Media Age,* W.W. Norton, 1st edition, 1980.

Barilleaux, Ryan J. and Randall E. Adkins, In "The Nominations: Process and Patterns," *The Elections of 1992,* 1st edition, CQ Press, 1993:21-56.

Benedetto, Richard, "Electorally a Big Lead for Clinton," *USA Today,* October 30, 1992:4A.

Benjamin, Alfred, *The Helping Interview,* Houghton Mifflin Company, 1st edition, 1974.

Bennett, W. Lance, *The Governing Crisis: Media, Money, and Marketing in American Elections,* St. Martin's Press, 1st edition, 1992.

Berelson, B., P. Lazarsfeld, and W. McPhee, *Voting,* University of Chicago Press, 1st edition, 1954.

Bernick, E. Lee and David J. Pratto, "Improving the Quality of Information in Mail Surveys: Use of Special Mailings," *Social Science Quarterly,* 75:1, March 1994: 212-219.

Black, Earl and Merle Black, *The Vital South: How Presidents Are Elected,* 1st edition, Harvard University Press, 1992.

Black, Earl and Merle Black, *The Vital South: How Presidents Are Elected,* Harvard University Press,1st edition, 1992.

Bledsoe, W. Craig, Instructor's Manual for *The Elections of 1992,* CQ Press, 1993.

Broder, David S. "Holding Their Feet to the Deficit Fire," *Washington Post National Weekly,* August 3-9,1992:4.

Broder, David S. "Bush's Problem Exposed," *Washington Post National Weekly,* February 24 - March 1, 1992:4.

Broder, David S. "Dan Quayle, Voice of Reason," *Washington Post National Weekly,* March 23-29,1992:4.

Broder, David S. and Thomas B. Edsall, "Post Mortem on New Hampshire," *Washington Post National Weekly,* February 24-March 1, 1992:6.

Burns, James MacGregor, *The Power to Lead: The Crisis of the American Presidency,* Simon and Schuster, 1st edition, 1984.

Campbell, A., P. Converse, W. Miller, and D. Stokes, *The American Voter,* Wiley Press, 1st edition, 1960.

Cannon, Carl M. and Kristin Huckshorn, "Perot Campaign Unraveled Behind Closed Doors," *The State,* July 19,1992:5D.

Carter, Bill "Murphy Brown Plans Revenge on Quayle," *The State,* July 21, 1992:5D.

Carullo, Julie J. *South Carolina Statistical Abstract,* South Carolina State Budget and Control Board - Division of Research and Statistical Services, 1993.

Ceasar, James W. *Reforming the Reforms: A Critical Analysis of the Presidential Selection Process,* Ballinger Publishing, 1st edition, 1982.

Ceasar, James W. *Presidential Selection: Theory and Development,* Princeton University Press, 1st edition, 1979.

Cole, Kyle and Sonya Forte Duhé "The Music Industry and Young Voters: The Impact of 'Rock the Vote' and 'Choose or Lose' on the Political Socialization of 18-24 Year Olds," A paper presented at the Southwest Social Science Association Meeting, New Orleans, Louisiana, March 17-20, 1993.

Collier, Ken and Stuart L. Escrock, "Who Gets What from the Networks? Network Coverage of the 1992 Presidential Primaries," A paper presented at the Southwest Social Science Association Meeting, New Orleans, Louisiana, March 17-20, 1993.

Crouse, Timothy, *The Boys on the Bus: Riding with the Campaign Press Corps,* Random House, 2nd edition, 1973.

Dahl, Robert A. *A Preface to Democratic Theory,* University of Chicago Press, 1st edition, 1956.

Dallek, Robert, "The Presidency: Mean to Me," *The Boston Sunday Globe,* May 15, 1994: 73,76.

Demick, Barbara and Robert A. Rankin, "Perot Supporters Taking Pride in Making 'Crazy' Impact on Race," *The State*, November 4, 1992:7A.

Devroy, Ann "The White House in Disarray," *Washington Post National Weekly*, November 25-December 1, 1991:6-7.

Devroy, Ann and John E. Yang, "For Bush a Quick Shove into Plan B," *Washington Post National Weekly*, February 24-March 1, 1992:8.

Devroy, Ann "Besieged, Battered & Bewildered," *Washington Post National Weekly*, July 13-19, 1992:12.

Diamond, Edwin, *The Media Show: The Changing Face of the News 1985-1990* MIT Press, 1st edition, 1991.

Diamond, Edwin and Stephen Bates, *The Spot: The Rise of Political Advertising on Television,* MIT Press, 3rd edition, 1992.

Dillman, Don A. *Mail and Telephone Surveys: The Total Design Method,* John Wiley and Sons, 1st edition, 1978.

Dowd, Maureen "Bush's Effort: Too Little, Too Late," *The State*, November 8, 1992:4D.

Drew, Dan and David Weaver, "Media Attention, Media Exposure, and Media Effects," *Journalism Quarterly* 67:4, 1990:740-748.

"Election '92 Highlights," *The State*, November 4, 1992:1A.

Entman, Robert M. *Democracy Without Citizens: Media and the Decay of American Politics,* Oxford University Press, 1st edition, 1989.

Epstein, Leon D. *Political Parties in the American Mold,* University of Wisconsin Press, 1st edition, 1986.

Euchner, Charles C. and John Anthony Maltese, *Selecting the President: From Washington to Bush,* 1st edition, CQ Press, 1992.

"Exit Polls: Who Voted and What Was Important," *The State*, November 4, 1992:7A.

Fedler, Fred, Tim Counts and Lowndes F. Stephens, "Newspaper Endorsements and Voter Behavior in the 1980 Presidential Election," *Newspaper Research Journal* 4, 1:3-12.

FitzSimon, Martha, "An Uncertain Season: Reporting in the Postprimary Period," *The Media and Campaign '92,* The Freedom Forum Media Studies Center, Columbia University, September, 1992.

FitzSimon, Martha, "Covering the Presidential Primaries," *The Media and Campaign '92,* The Freedom Forum Media Studies Center, Columbia University, June, 1992.

FitzSimon, Martha, "The Finish Line: Covering the Campaigns's Final Days," *The Media and Campaign '92,* The Freedom Forum Media Studies Center, Columbia University, January, 1993.

FitzSimon, Martha and Edward Pease, "The Homestretch: New Politics. New Media. New Voters?," *The Media and Campaign '92,* The Freedom Forum Media Studies Center, Columbia University, October, 1992.

Flanigan, William H. and Nancy Zingale, *Political Behavior of the American Electorate,* CQ Press, 7th edition, 1991.

Germond, Jack W. and Jules Witcover, *Mad As Hell: Revolt at the Ballot Box 1992,* Warner Books, 1993.

Germond, Jack W. and Jules Witcover, *Whose Broad Stripes and Bright Stars? The Trivial Pursuit of the Presidency in 1988,* 1st edition, Warner Books, 1989.

Gillespie, J. David,*Politics at the Periphery: Third Parties in Two-Pary America,* The University of South Carolina Press, 1st edition, 1993.

Gillespie, J. David, *Politics at the Periphery: Third Parties in Two-Party America,* 1st edition, The University of South Carolina Press, 1993.

Goldstein, Tom, *The News at Any Cost,* Simon and Schuster, 1st edition, 1986.

Gordon, Raymond L. *Interviewing Strategy, Techniques, and Tactics,* Dorsey Press, 1st edition, 1969.

Graber, Doris A. *Processing The News: How People Tame the Information Tide,* Longman, 1st edition, 1988.

Graber, Doris A. *Processing The News: How People Tame the Information Tide,* 2nd edition, Longman, Inc., 1988.

Graber, Doris A. *Processing the News: How People Tame the Information Tide,* Longman Inc., 1st edition, 1984.

Green, Charles "Official Fired After Passport Searches," *The State,* November 11, 1992:11A

Gunther, Marc "Voters Turned Off by Negative Ads," *The State,* October 21, 1993:9A.

Hart, Roderick, *The Sound of Leadership,* University of Chicago Press, 1st edition, 1987.

Hellweg, Susan A., Michael Pfau, and Steven R. Brydon, *Televised Presidential Debates: Advocacy in Contemporary America,* Praegar Publishing, 1st edition, 1992.

Herman, Edward S. and Noam Chomsky, *Manufacturing Consent: The Political Economy of the Mass Media,* Pantheon Books, 1st edition, 1988.

Hershey, Marjorie Randon, "The Campaign and the Media," In *The Election of 1988: Reports and Interpretations,* 1st edition, Chatham House Publishers, 1989.

Hershey, Marjorie Randon "The Constructed Explanation: Interpreting Election Results in the 1984 Presidential Race," *Journal of Politics,* 54:4, November, 1992:943-976.

Hoffman, Mark S. *World Almanac and Book of Facts 1993,* Pharos Books, 1st edition, 1992.

Isikoff, Michael and Ann Devroy "Two New Recruits Join the Cause," Washington Post National Weekly, June 8-14,1992:15.

Jacobson, Gary "Congress: Unusual Year, Unusual Election," *The Elections of 1992,* CQ Press, 1993:153-182.

Jamieson, Kathleen H., and Karlyn Kohrs Campbell, *The Interplay of Influence,* Wadsworth Publishing, 1st edition, 1983.

Jamieson, Kathleen H., and David S. Birdswell, *Presidential Debates: The Challenge of Creating an Informed Electorate,* Oxford University Press, 1st edition, 1988.

Jamieson, Kathleen H., *Packaging the Presidency: A History and Criticism of Presidential Campaign Advertising,* Oxford University Press, 2nd edition, 1992.

Johnson, Janet Buttolph and Richard A. Joslyn, *Political Science Research Methods,* CQ Press, 1st edition, 1986.

Kaid, Lynda et al, "Television News and Presidential Campaigns: The Legitimization of Televised Political Advertising," *Social Science Quarterly,* vol. 74, no. 2, June 1993:274-285.

Kane, Eileen, *Doing Your Own Research: How to do basic descriptive research in the social sciences and humanities,* Marion Boyars, 2nd edition, 1985.

Keen, Judy "Bush Faces 'Sleaze Factor,'" USA Today, August 12, 1992:1-2A.

Kellerman, Donald S. "The Campaign and The Press at Halftime," Supplement to the July/August, 1992 *Columbia Journalism Review.*

Kessel, John, Presidential Campaign Politics, Dorsey Press, 1st edition, 1984.

Key, V.O.,Jr. *The Responsible Electorate,* Harvard University Press, 1st edition, 1966.

Kohurt, Andrew "The Press and Campaign '92: A Self-Assessment," Supplement to the March/April, 1993 *Columbia Journalism Review.*

Krippendorff, Klaus Content Analysis: An Introduction to Its Methodology, Sage Publications, 1st edition, 1980.

Kurtz, Howard, *Media Circus: The Trouble with America's Newspapers,* Times Books, 1st edition, 1993.

Kurtz, Howard "Are Media Smitten with Clinton?," *The State* September 2, 1992:5A.

Ladd, Carll Everett, *Where Have All the Voters Gone? The Fracturing of America's Political Parties,* W.W. Norton & Company, 1st edition, 1978.

Ladd, Everett C. *The Ladd Report,* 4th Edition, Volume 1, W.W. Norton and Company, 1991.

Lauter, David "Clinton Team Outplanned G.O.P.," *The State,* November 8, 1992:4D.

Lazarsfeld, P., B. Berelson, and H. Gaudet, *The People's Choice,* Duell, Sloan & Pearce, 1st edition, 1944.

"Liberal Iowa Senator Becomes 3rd to Seek Presidency," *The State*, September 16, 1991.

Lichtenberg, Judith, "The Politics of Character and the Character of Journalism," Discussion Paper D-2, Barone Center for the Press, Politics, and Public Policy, Harvard University, October 1989.

Lowery, Shearon A. and Melvin L. DeFleur, *Milestones in Mass Communication Research,* Longman Press, 1st edition, 1983.

Lowi, Theodore, *The Personal President,* Cornell University Press, 1st edition, 1985.

Manoff, Robert Karl, and Michael Scudson, *Reading The News,* Pantheon Books, 1st edition, 1986.

Maraniss, David and Bill McAllister "Just When He Thought the Worst Was Behind Him," *Washington Post National Weekly*, February 24-March 1, 1992:13-14.

Markus, Gregory B. "The Impact of Personal and National Economic Conditions on the Presidential Vote: A Pooled Cross-Sectional Analysis," *American Journal of Political Science,* 32, 1988:137-154.

Markus, Gregory B. "Political Attitudes During an Election Year: A Report on the 1980 NES Panel Study," *American Political Science Review,* 76, 1982:538-560.

Matalin, Mary and James Carville, *All's Fair: Love, War, and Running For President,* 1st edition, Simon and Schuster, 1994.

McCubbins, Matthew D., *Under The Watchful Eye: Managing Presidential Campaigns in the Television Era,* CQ Press, 1992.

McGrory, Mary "GOP is in No Mood to Party," *Washington Post National Weekly*, August 3-9,1992:25.

Minz, John "Who is Ross Perot?," *Washington Post National Weekly*, May 4-10, 1992:6-8.

Neuman, W. Russell, *The Future of the Mass Audience,* Cambridge University Press, 1991.

Neuman, W.R., *The Paradox of Mass Politics,* Harvard University Press, 1st edition, 1986.

"New Clinton Ad to Begin Airing Today," *The State*, August 31, 1992:3A.

Noelle-Newman, Elisabeth, *The Spiral of Silence: Public Opinion - Our Social Skin,* University of Chicago Press, 1st edition, 1984.

Norman, Jim "Where Those Poll Figures Come From," *USA Today*, October 30, 1992:4A.

Norrander, Barbara, *Super Tuesday: Regional Politics and Presidential Primaries*, 1st edition, The University Press of Kentucky, 1992.

Noyes, Richard E., S. Robert Lichter, and Daniel R. Amundson, "Was TV Election News Better This Time? A Content Analysis of 1988 and 1992 Campaign Coverage," *Journal of Political Science,* Volume 21, 1993:3-25.

Ornstein, Norman, Andrew Kohut, and Larry McCarthy, *The People, the Press & Politics: The Times Mirror Study of the American Electorate,* 1st edition, Addison-Wesley Publishing, Inc., 1988.

Owen, Diana, *Media Messages in American Presidential Elections,* Greenwood Press, 1st edition, 1991.

Page, Benjamin, *Choices and Echoes in Presidential Elections: Rational Man and Electoral Democracy,* University of Chicago Press, 5th edition, 1982.

Parenti, Michael, *Inventing Reality: The Politics of the Mass Media,* St Martin's Press, 2nd edition, 1993.

Patterson, Thomas E., *Out of Order: How the decline of political parties and the growing power of the news media undermine the American way of electing presidents,* Alfred A. Knopf, Inc., 1993.

Patterson, Thomas E. *The Mass Media Election,* Praeger Publishing, 1st edition, 1980.

Phillips, Kevin P. *Media-cracy: American Parties and Politics in the Communications Age,* 1st edition, Doubleday and Company, 1975.

Phillips, Kevin P. *Media-cracy: American Parties and Politics in the Communications Age,* Doubleday and Company, 1st edition, 1975.

Phillips, Kevin *The Politics of Rich and Poor: Wealth and the American Electorate in the Reagan Electorate,* Random House, 1st edition, 1990.

Polsby, Nelson W. *The Consequences of Party Reform,* Oxford University Press, 1st edition, 1983.

Pomper, Gerald M. et al, *The Election of 1992,* Chatham House, 1st edition, 1993.

Pomper, Gerald M. et al, *The Election of 1988: Reports and Interpretations,* Chatham House, 1st edition, 1989.

Popkin, Samuel L. *The Reasoning Voter: Communication and Persuasion in Presidential Campaigns,* University of Chicago Press, 1st edition, 1991.

Postman, Neil and Steve Powers, *How To Watch TV News,* Penguin Books, 1st edition, 1993.

Press, Charles and Kenneth Verburg, *American Politicians and Journalists,* Scott, Foresman and Company, 1st edition, 1988.

Quirk, Paul J. and Jon K. Dalager, "The Election: A New Democrat, In" *The Elections of 1992, 1st* edition, CQ Press, 1993.

Raum, Tom "Voter's Questions Fuel 2nd Debate," *The State,* October 16, 1992:1A.

Robinson, Michael J. and Margaret A. Sheehan, *Over the Wire and On TV,* Sage Publications, 1st edition, 1983.

Robinson, Michael J. and Margaret A. Sheehan, *Over the Wire and On TV,* Sage Publications, 1st edition, 1983.

Rosenstiel, Thomas B. "Media Vow Political Coverage Beyond Soundbite," *The State,* December 8, 1991:4D.

Sabato, Larry J., *Feeding Frenzy: How Attack Journalism Has Transformed American Politics,* The Free Press, 1991.

Sabato, Larry J. *Feeding Frenzy: How Attack Journalism Has Transformed American Politics,* The Free Press, 1st edition, 1991.

Sabato, Larry J. *Feeding Frenzy: How Attack Journalism Has Transformed American Politics,* 1st edition, The Free Press, 1991.

Salmore, Stephen A. and Barbara Salmore, *Candidates, Parties, and Campaigns: Electoral Politics in America,* CQ Press, 1st edition, 1985.

Schnattschneider, E.E., *Party Government,* Rinehart, 1st edition, 1942.

Schram, Martin, *The Great American Video Game: Presidential Politics in the Television Age,* William Morrow and Company, 1st edition, 1987.

Scoppe, Cindi Ross "White Voters Gave Bush His S.C. Win," *The State,* November 6, 1993:1A.

ShoeMaker, Pamela J. and Stephen D. Reese, "Exposure to What? Integrating Media Content and Effects," *Journalism Quarterly,* 64:4, Winter 1990: 649-652.

Shogan, Robert "Bush Plans New Attack on Character," *The State,* October 19,1993:1A.

Smith, Ted J. III, *The Vanishing Economy: Television Coverage of Economic Affairs 1982-1987,* Media Institute, 1988.

State, A Knight-Ridder Newspaper, Columbia, South Carolina, July 1 to November 3, 1992.

Staten, Clifford L. and G. Sam Sloss, "The Media and Politics: A Content Analysis of the *Louisville Courier-Journal* During the 1992 Presidential Election," *Journal of Political Science,* Volume 21, 1993:90-102.

Strate, John M., Coit Cook Ford III, and Thomas B. Jankowski, "Women's Use of the Print Media to Follow Politics," *Social Science Quarterly,* 75:1, March 1994: 166-186.

Strate, John M., Coit Cook Ford III, and Thomas B. Jankowski, "Women's Use of Print Media to Follow Politics," *Social Science Quarterly,* 75:1, March 1994:166-186.

Sudman, Seymour and Norman M. Bradburn *Asking Questions: A Practical Guide to Questionnaire Design,* Jossey-Bass Publishers, 1st edition, 1982.

Sundquist, James L. *Dynamics of the Party System: Alignment and Realignment of Political Parties in the United States,* The Brookings Institution, 1st edition, 1973.

Swansbrough, Robert H. and David M. Brodsky *The South's New Politics: Realignment and Dealignment,* University of South Carolina Press, 1st edition, 1988.

"Television News Index and Abstracts," Vanderbilt Television News Archive, 110 21st Avenue South, Suite 704, Nashville, Tennessee, July, August, September, October, November, 1992.

Taylor, Paul, *See How They Run: Electing the President in an Age of Mediaocracy,* Alfred A. Knopf, 1st edition, 1990.

Tullis, Jeffery, *The Rhetorical President,* Princeton University Press, 1st edition, 1987.

Warwick, Donald P. and Charles A. Lininger *The Sample Survey: Theory and Practice,* McGraw-Hill, 1st edition, 1975.

Wayne, Stephen J. *The Road to the White House 1992,* St. Martin's Press, 1st edition, 1992.

Wayne, Stephen J. and Clyde Wilcox, *The Quest for National Office: Readings on Elections,* St. Martin's Press, 1st edition, 1992.

Westin, Av *News-Watch: How TV Decides the News,* Simon and Schuster, 1st edition, 1982.

Whitman, David "Beyond the Riot Epicenter," *U.S. News & World Report,* May 31, 1993:55.

Williams, Juan "Creating a New, Improved Clinton," Washington Post National Weekly, July 13-19,1992:7.

Wilson, Douglas L. "Thomas Jefferson and the Character Issue," in *Atlantic Monthly,* vol. 270, no. 5, November 1992: 57-74.

Winebrenner, Hugh, *The Iowa Precinct Caucuses: The Making of a Media Event,* Iowa State University Press, 1st edition, 1987.

WIS-TV News, local NBC affiliate, Columbia, South Carolina, 11:00 pm. news broadcasts July 1 to November 3, 1992.

Index